SPIRIT WHEEL

SPIRIT
WHEEL

MEDITATIONS FROM AN
INDIGENOUS ELDER

STEVEN CHARLESTON

Broadleaf Books
Minneapolis

SPIRIT WHEEL
Meditations from an Indigenous Elder

Library of Congress Control Number 2022050861 (print)

Cover design: Juicebox Designs

Print ISBN: 978-1-5064-8665-9
eBook ISBN: 978-1-5064-8666-6
Printed in China

For the okla tikba

CONTENTS

INTRODUCTION   I

I
TRADITION OF THE ANCESTORS   15

II
KINSHIP WITH CREATION   77

III
VISION OF THE SPIRIT   131

IV
BALANCE OF LIFE   197

THE FIFTH DIRECTION   255

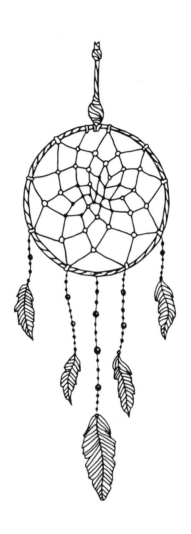

INTRODUCTION

SPINNING THE FOUR DIRECTIONS

I sing here at the midnight hour,
Chanting prayers beneath the moon.
I have no gift to give but kindness,
No wisdom but compassion
No authority but our shared experience.

Like you I have watched the seasons turn,
Deep cycles of change
Blessings and sorrows mixed
In the many colors of our lives.

What is spiritual is what is most ordinary,
The common threads of hope and mercy
The things we know best
Because we have lived them all.
So I chant the turn of another day,
Spinning grace into the world
Spinning the four directions until they turn like a wheel.

A mystery lives at the heart of this book.
Over a decade ago I began writing down what came into my mind each day after prayer. I am an elder, a Native American, and I have been consciously engaged in the spiritual life since I was four years old. I began this spirit life in an extended family in rural Oklahoma, where my family had arrived long ago on the Trail of Tears: the forced removal of my people, the Choctaw Nation, from our homeland in what is now the southeastern United States. Thousands of our people died on that death march, and I was raised to remember their courage and sacrifice. I was brought up in the story of our people, the story of our ancestors, the okla tikba, and the vision that sustained them through generations of struggle and hope.

Prayer, therefore, was as natural for me as breathing. My great-grandfather and grandfather were both hattak holitopa: holy men, preachers of the word. Their legacy in our family was strong. As a child I was told that one day I would grow up to be like them. I would live a life of the Spirit. I took this expectation seriously and believed in the traditions of my people.

As the years went by, I found myself living between two spiritual worlds: the traditional faith of America's Indigenous people and the Christian faith, one of the major religious teachings of the larger society. When I became an adolescent, I began a quest to find the place where I belonged between these two ancient visions. I brought my Indigenous faith with me as I began exploring one Christian denomination after another. I went to Jewish and Baha'i communities as well. My search was simple: I would go to worship with any faith community, without preconception or judgment, to experience their way of praying. If I did not feel a connection, I would move on to the next community. If I felt a spiritual resonance I would go back, and keep going back, until I was sure this was not the right fit for me.

I don't know how many different communities I tried, but as many as were possible for a teenager with a car in Oklahoma City. Baptist, Methodist, Roman Catholic, Unitarian, Orthodox, Presbyterian, Reform Judaism, Pentecostal: the list was long, and the adventure of exploration was a major part of my spiritual growth into adulthood. I listened and learned. I came to appreciate the many shades of human faith.

One day I walked into a very small Episcopal mission on the edge of town. The priest at this little church was a man who had been broken and brought back to life. He was an alcoholic who had almost died alone on the floor of a cheap motel. The fact that he survived and was given a second chance he attributed to the unconditional love of a higher power. It was not the theology or the ceremony of his church that captured my heart as much as it was his personal honesty and humility. Those qualities rang true for me as a Native American believer, because they are the same qualities we value in our traditional medicine people. This man was a living bridge between the two sides of my spiritual experience. He lived what he preached.

Yet even his example was not enough to reconcile the history between my people and the Christian missionary experience in America. For a time, the Episcopal Church gave me a place to carry on my search for answers, for meaning, for a faith that was both local to my culture and universal in hope for the whole world. I went to Trinity College in Connecticut as a religion student. I went to seminary in Cambridge, Massachusetts. I studied many religions and many historical periods. I did my research in the Western style of academic rigor and critical study. But in the end, they were not enough. Something was still missing.

I needed to do as much learning in my Native tradition as I had done in the European religious academy. So once again, I set out on a quest to find where I belonged. I went out into the Indigenous world, both here and abroad, out into the ancient wisdom of the okla tikba. As I had done with Western churches, so I did with my own Native tradition. I visited as many Indigenous communities as I could: Kiowa, Inuit, Hopi, Cree, Lakota, Navajo, Athabascan, Pequot, Arapahoe, Ojibway, and many more. The list was long, and this quest took years. I was welcomed by Native Hawaiians, Maoris in Aotearoa/New Zealand, and Aborigines of Australia. I met with people of the Amazon in Brazil. I sat with the elders and listened. I attended their ceremonies and joined in their prayers. I stayed with families and took my part in daily life. Little by little I immersed myself in the collective wisdom of generations of Indigenous people. My respect of their vision grew ever deeper.

For more than seventy years now I have followed my quest, my search for understanding. Over these years it has expanded to include Buddhism, Hinduism, Taoism, Islam, Shinto, and many other faiths. Now I am an elder myself. A faithful follower of my Native way, but also a spiritual traveler who has learned much from many good people—people like you, who want to know where they came from, where they are going, and where they belong.

And that is the mystery of this book. Somehow, I believe, the words you find here will speak to you. They will not only make sense; they will rise up out of your own experience. They will not be telling you something you did not know but rather something that has been part of you forever. The brief messages I have received and written for more than a decade seem to speak that rare language of a local culture with a universal meaning. Somehow these little messages speak to everyone alike. They cross all frontiers and cultures. I know this because since the very first message came to me, I have written them down on Facebook for all the world to see. And the response I have received over these many years has been both humbling and inspirational. People from every point of the compass, from many faith traditions and many countries, have embraced what you will read here. They have let me know that these little messages give them encouragement, strength, and confidence in our shared future. My messages rise out of the rich soil of Native America's ancient faith, rooted in many tribes and nations. But their branches spread out to touch people of all walks of life, of all hopes and all dreams.

How is that possible? How does that happen? Who is really the author of what you are about to read? Why is this happening now?

There are many mysteries in this small book—mysteries that I believe can only be solved by reading and rereading the messages here. Read them in the context of your own faith, but with a curiosity, an openness, to hear what Native America has to say, to teach, to share. There is spiritual healing in this book, and there may even be an enlightenment. Only you will be able to tell. When you enter into the mystery of these words for yourself, do so without preconception or judgment. With honesty and humility. Enter the deep earth of our ancient longing and reach for the highest branches of our collective hope.

To help you make that quest, let me offer a simple orientation to what you will find here. First, this book is called *Chanaha Shilombish—Spirit Wheel*—because that image is the spiritual metaphor that holds this whole experience together. In these pages I refer to the Spirit as the higher power that rescued my priest friend so long ago—that found him in that seedy motel, that brought him back to life as a compassionate and loving person. You may call the Spirit by whatever name you choose in your own faith, but here the word *Spirit* will mean that Great Mystery my ancestors always acknowledged: a vast unseen consciousness, both wise and compassionate, that has created all there is and watches over that creation with unconditional love.

The Wheel is life. It is the reality we all inhabit together: the ever-changing, ever-transforming reality in which we all live. My ancestors called it, at various times, the medicine wheel, the hoop of the nations, the great circle of existence. We are all on that ever-turning wheel—all of creation, people and animals, animate and inanimate, rocks and trees, the whole universe. The Wheel is the mystery both behind and within creation. It is the meaning and purpose the Spirit first intended when the lights went on in a dark void.

When I started writing these messages—writing down what came into my heart after prayer, day after day, year after year, season after season—I did not realize how they would help me find my place on the Spirit Wheel. I wanted a place to belong. I wanted a vision that would make sense. At the time I began writing these messages, I did not realize how my own quest would reconcile the faith of the okla tikba to the many traditions of other cultures from around the world. I did not appreciate how the spiritual path of my ancestors had something wonderful, something powerful, to share with people of all walks of life. But it did. And it does: the mystery of how we can all speak the same language even if we use different words.

In my tradition we call that universal vision the Four Directions. This means that the Spirit Wheel is not one tradition or one direction but many traditions, the spiritual reality that encompasses us all. As I have read and reread the messages you will find here, I have come to realize that the Four Directions are woven like threads through them all. I did not see that at first, but now it is clear to me, and I have gathered the messages I wrote into the Four Directions so it will be easier for you to see as well.

The four hallmarks of Native American spirituality are Tradition, Kinship, Vision, Balance.

We honor the wisdom of our ancestors: Tradition.

We recognize our interrelatedness with all living things: Kinship.

We seek the eternal Spirit in the here and now: Vision.

We walk in faith with spiritual mindfulness: Balance.

This book gathers the messages I have received and seek to share into one of these Four Directions. That will help you explore their meaning. At times the connection between the message you are reading and one of the Four Directions may seem clear, but at other times it may take a little more reflection to make the association. The Four Directions here are not rigid categories, but porous and liminal enclosures to suggest where each message appears on the Spirit Wheel. Take each message as you find it. Let it speak to you directly. Ponder its meaning. But see it in relation to other messages in its place on the Wheel. Then the vision of the entire Wheel may become more apparent to you, in that breathtaking moment when insight becomes an invitation to wonder.

At the conclusion of this book, on the other side of the Four Directions, I write a few words about what it all means, the same questions that started me on my journey as a child: the pursuit of a great mystery. Why am I here? Where do I belong? Where am I going? In the last chapter I give a brief commentary on where the Wheel is taking us and why it is important that we all go together. I look ahead, with an old man's eyes, to see the shape of what will be: the Fifth Direction of hope and transcendence.

There are wheels within wheels in this book. Mysteries within mysteries. A lifetime search. A vision both local and universal. A wisdom as ancient as creation and as young as tomorrow. I am grateful you are on the Spirit Wheel with me. I hope these small messages will unlock your mystery as much as they have unlocked mine.

I
TRADITION OF
THE ANCESTORS

TO TURN THE WHEEL OF HISTORY

To each generation a task is given,
By a will and purpose greater than our own
A work to be accomplished,
Even without knowing the outcome.

We are called, as if by an instinct of migration
Something deep in our collective subconscious,
A summons to see the moment clearly
To understand the implications, and then to respond
To act in order to change, to turn the wheel of history,
To save what must be preserved.

Now is our time. This is our calling.
We see the need. We know the consequences.
Let us be about what must be done.

GOOD MEDICINE

In the tradition of Native America
We speak not only of the good news
But of the good medicine.

This medicine is the power of the sacred to heal our lives
To put right whatever may be wrong for us.
It is the spiritual force of love.
Good medicine is both a presence in our lives
And an active energy that moves around us.

Today I pray that my ancestors may share
Their good medicine with each of you.
I pray that the Spirit, the source of all good medicine
May release its authority into your life
And through you pass its healing
To touch those you love.

TIMELESS WIND

I walked among lost graves
To hear my ancestors speak
Whispering beneath the branches
As the timeless wind passed by.

The faith we leave is the faith we live
The faith we learn the faith we give.

Some seek to hide an emptiness within
Others listen to truth among the poor
Touch truth on bodies broken and know truth
As the timeless wind passes by.

OUR ANCESTORS

I have seen them walking by night
That long procession of the ancient faithful
Our ancestors.

Over the darkened hills they come
Each holding a glowing light
A winding stream of glowing light
A shared voice of hushed praise
A chant rising to the watching moon:
Our ancestors.
The ageless ones who bless unseen.

They keep their vigil for all the living
For every soul.
They pray for us. They watch over us.
They intercede for every need.

Where they walk peace follows.
When they pray even angels bow their heads.

BLESS THE DOUBTERS

Spirit, bless the doubters
The ones who read the fine print
Before they sign the contract of life.

Spirit, bless those who question religion
And demand that it be as transparent as its teaching.

Bless the ones who are not fooled by titles
But want to know what is being done.
These voices speak a truth faith needs to hear.

They hold the holy accountable to practice what we preach.
Better a doubt with integrity than a belief without it.

SCHOLAR OF THE SENSES

For all the great thoughts I have read
For all the deep books I have studied
None has brought me nearer to Spirit
Than a walk beneath shimmering leaves

Golden red with the fire of autumn
When the air is crisp
And the sun a pale eye, watching.

I am a scholar of the senses
A theologian of the tangible.

Spirit touches me and I touch Spirit
Each time I lift a leaf from my path
A thin flake of fire golden red
Still warm from the breath that made it.

LET EVENING FIND ME

It is a good day to live.

My ancestors were unafraid to make the spirit journey
When the time came
Accepting it as a good day to die.

They saw every other day as a good day to live.

Let me embrace each dawn as gift.
Let me walk the hours of day unafraid
With grace and faith unbounded.
Let evening find me close to those I love
Warming my soul by the fires of their laughter.

Let me sleep believing tomorrow will be a blessing.

SLOW THE CLOCK

I caught myself wanting to stop time again.
It happens more and more.

I go about my ordinary day
And suddenly I have this longing
To slow the clock
To keep things as they are
If only for a while.

I am an old man getting younger.
I have learned again what I knew as a child:
Days are magic, nights are mystery.

The younger I become, the more I want to play
Just for a little longer.
Before I hear my Mother's call.
Before I have to sleep.

A BORROWED LIFE

I live a borrowed life on loan from the Spirit.

One day my words will be forgotten.
My voice an echo drifting on an ocean breeze.
Images of me will be dust,
My most precious possessions powder.
Even those tied to me by the double helix
Will not recall my name.

But I do not despair of my short span
Or wish my memory immortal.

The One who loaned me this life will not forget.
The Spirit will come to claim it, calling me by name
A borrowed life returned, redeemed by endless love.

THE DIGNITY OF THE QUESTION

I have stood on the edge of a midnight canyon
And called out my question into silent shadows: Why?

Why suffering? Why pain?
Why the hurt that haunts our lives?
Why the wrong that overwhelms the good?

I get no answer, only an echo.
I will go on asking
Until the next generation of questioners takes my place.
Suffering will not have the last word
Not without challenge.

We may not know the reason
But we will have the dignity of the question.

THE ANCIENT LIGHT

Once in Alaska, long ago on a winter night
Darker than any darkness I have known
The light I carried failed
And I was alone with that most ancient fear
The one that haunted us before there was fire.

Disoriented, I knew if I walked the wrong way
I might go on walking forever
Wearing the night like a shroud.
I prayed into the icy wind
Sent out streamers of breath like a lifeline.

Then I saw a light, a single light
A cabin light just beyond the trees.
The Spirit is the light that comes to us
When we need it most
The ancient light that calms our fear
The hope as old as fire.

A PASSING PRAYER

The hour will come, the time of my passing.

I do not know when or how.
I do not know if I will be surprised or relieved or aware.
I only know that one day I will stand
With my back to what has been
And my face toward what I will discover.

When that moment arrives
I pray a simple passing prayer:
Receive me as I am, O Spirit
As trusting in your kindness
As when I first breathed
The breath you gave me.

Forgive my faults
Reveal my learnings
Bless those I leave behind.
Let my love redeem what is past
And welcome what is to come.

BLESSED ARE YOU

The meditations of my heart
Are the words I write each morning.
Guided by unseen currents in the stillness of prayer
Scribbling quietly before the dawn
To catch the meaning waiting
At the far edge of every night.

I do not know how well these words will serve
The purpose to which they are printed
But truth is never tame and justice never content.

So I write what my heart reveals:
Blessed are you
Who believe without judgment
Who love without condition
Who act without reward
Who give without prompting
Who pray without ceasing
Who keep on dancing
When there is no music.

AFLAME

The candles where I pray flicker to life one by one
Each a small universe of hope in itself
Bravely aflame with the desire to be fulfilled
Glowing against the dark as if saying I am here.

I am here, let me live. I am here, let me dream
Let me grow, let me become.

I light my candles because they embody
Not only the prayers but the person.
They are the spark of life within each of us
Flickering within the air of the Spirit
Shining into the cold expanse of space
Repeating the ancient message: I am here.

SEEK

Seek wisdom from the elders
Older souls who have seen,
Remembered, understood.

Seek strength from your peers
Companions on the same path
Those who know without explanation.

Seek renewal from the youth
Young spirits alive with possibility
Alert to honesty.

Seek nurture from children
Innocent visionaries
Truth tellers without ambition.

Seek love from your ancestors
Those rare spirits who can fly beside you
The trusted ones of your heart.

Seek truth from the unseen Spirit
The conscience more true than law
The voice that knows your name.

ONCE AND ALWAYS

You are embraced by a love so deep
No force among the far-flung stars
Can separate you from it.

Not illness. Not sorrow.
Not even death.

You cannot fall. You cannot be lost.
You are once and always held in arms
That do more than shelter you.
They are the embrace of life itself
The warmth of a sun so pure
Its light dazzles the imagination
With a clarity of grace
Beyond the reach of any shadow.

Nothing can harm you. You are safe.
The power of the Spirit surrounds you.
The love of the Spirit protects you.
The peace of the Spirit is within you
And will abide there forever.

OUR OWN WAY

Like you, I pray in my own way.

I place my offering into the open hand of Mother Earth
A small sprinkling of tobacco
Swept away on the feathered wind.
I look to the face of the sky
The mirror behind which generations
Of my ancestors stand, watching.

I recite quiet prayers to the compass points of the horizon
The four directions, the borders of time in which we live.

Within the circle of corn pollen on which I stand
I draw all of life as closely as I can,
Humbled to be taking breath
Blessed this day by the Spirit who loves us all
And listens when we pray
Each in our own way.

MENDING THE CIRCLE

From four sacred directions, I saw the elders assemble
Winter-haired wisdom, come to speak by evening fires
Before night could claim the light for the stars alone.

From four sacred directions, the people came
To hear the ancient stories, to sing the ancient songs
Before dawn could claim their voice for the wind alone.

From four sacred directions, the spirits gathered
Love to bind our wounds, hope to heal our hearts
Faith to clear our minds, truth to set us free
Gathered by prayer, gathered by the Spirit
To mend the great circle
Before time could claim our vision for the past alone.

THE KIVA

We emerge into life.
That is the wisdom of my Native family
Who live in the kiva cultures of the Southwest.

The kiva is a holy space beneath the earth.
You climb out of it on a ladder.

To live again you begin by seeing the light above.
You make the effort to move up.
You emerge into the world again.
You feel the air and breathe.
You learn to walk once more.

Life is a process, a movement, an intention.
From below to above. From dark to light.
The kiva is the symbol for this truth.

We participate in our own birth, in our own healing,
In our own emergence.

WINTER TALK

For generations my ancestors said that
Cold days and nights were special
Because only during this season
Could the sacred stories be told.
They called it winter talk.

Gathered by the fire, the elders would spin the sagas
That were woven through the holy fabric of our lives
Passing on wisdom so old it had no beginning,
Even in their own memory.

Winter talk reminds us that we are a people of the Spirit
Sharing in a story as old as time, a living legacy of faith
That believes and by believing keeps the human story holy.
You are part of an ancient journey, one older than memory.

WHERE OUR PAST STILL LIVES

I am in a quiet place, embraced by a forest
Where my ancestors still walk beneath the light of day.

I have been listening to the old stories,
The memories of my people
Spoken in the old language,
The sounds of an ancient spirit.

I am learning. I am listening.
I am growing in wisdom and compassion.
We all have a place we can go where our past still lives.

We all have teachers who can share their memory with us.
We have a community that speaks our language.

Your past is the doorway into your future.
Your tradition is the memory
That shapes who you will one day be.

BE THE PEACE

Striving to live a spiritual life is not easy
But in Native American tradition it is simple.

Speak kindly about others,
Especially those with whom you disagree.
Give to help those in need
With both generosity and consistency.
Watch for the unexpected wisdom spoken
In word and deed.
Carry no prejudice toward any member
Of your human family.

Think of yourself as a healer and act accordingly.
Listen more than you speak.
Look for the treasure of humor and share it freely.

Ask always in prayer to do
What is most pleasing to the Spirit.
Consider every life to be of value.
Respect elders, honor youth, cherish children.
Be the peace in which you live each day.

WHAT I SAW AS A CHILD

When I was a child I thought of the world around me
As a magical place
With small spirits darting through my grandmother's garden
Like fireflies at night
Unseen voices whispering stories
From the branches of the old cottonwood tree
And angels flying over the house
To chase the billowing storm clouds away.

All of these images and a thousand more
Filled the spirit world in which I lived.

But now I am older.
So I have come to understand reality.
And what I understand is this:
I was absolutely right about what I saw as a child,
Because I still see it now.
I still live in a spirit world. I hope you do too.

PROPHET OF THE OBVIOUS

I am the herald of the ordinary
The mystic of the common
The prophet of the obvious.

Those descriptions make me smile
Because they remind me
That what is the most mystical
Is actually the most mundane.

We do not need to be transported to far distant realms
To catch a glimpse of the sacred.
If we spend all of our time with our head in the clouds
We may miss the Spirit who works in clay and water.

Faith does not begin in what we imagine
But in what we experience.
It is felt, held, passed on.
Heaven is not over the rainbow
But in the earth after the rain.

OUR MOTHER NEEDS US

The earth is holy. She is our sacred Mother.

For centuries before centuries my ancestors knew this
And lived beneath the shelter
Of her great forests and high mountains.

Today we still know it, even as she struggles to survive.

Our wisdom and respect are not inherent in our culture.
We honor the Mother not by some special gift
Of spiritual insight.
All cultures, all people, can learn to live
In harmony with the cycles of life.

It is simply a matter of practicing what we preach.
Let us determine to do so.
Our Mother needs us, calls to us.
Let every son and daughter stand up now
For what must be done to save her.

THE SOUL

Let me state my belief as simply and clearly as I can.
I believe you and I are more than water,
Chemicals, and electricity.

We are more than winners of a cosmic lottery
That grants life and consciousness at random
And only for a few brief years.

I believe in the soul,
That strange and wonderful mystery of the human spirit
The inner vibration we feel that resonates with our mind
A source of life that is older than the stars.

We are beings of a deep awareness:
Living memories of a time before time.

GIFT

I imagine many of us have small spiritual rituals
We perform each day
So often, in fact, that they become second nature.

One of mine occurs each morning.
When I first open my eyes, I say quietly,
"Thank you for giving me another day."

This helps me never to take a single day for granted
But to always acknowledge the mystery of life
Both around me and within me.

Life is a gift.
We may each recognize a different source for that gift
But we all can be thankful
For the simple joy of opening our eyes.

EVERY WOMAN

I am from a matrilineal culture.
We trace our families through the female line
And we take our mother's name.

For centuries women held positions of political
Economic and spiritual power in our society.
As their children, we are raised to honor and revere women
And respect them in thought, word, and deed.
Stories about the treatment of women
Make me think of my heritage.

I value the wisdom of women.
I wish I could wrap a star quilt
Around the shoulders of every woman
A sign of her nobility and a pledge of her safety.

WHEN MY TIME COMES

When my time comes, I will hear the distant drum
Call me to join the dance.

I will see my ancestors moving
In stately procession toward the dance ground
Taking their places in the never-ending circle
Dressed in their finest traditional attire
Majestic in their embodiment
Of all that our people have stood for
All that they have seen and dreamed
For twice ten thousand years.

Here, on the hills they called sacred
Here, in the birthplace of their truth and their courage.

When my time comes, I will join the dance
And scatter starlight with every step I take.

THE BACK OF THE PARADE

If the progress of humanity
Is one valiant march into the future
Self-confident in science and power,
Self-assured in creed and culture
Striding past the need for compromise or compassion
Then let me walk where I belong:
At the very back of that parade.

I will walk with the stragglers and the dreamers
The ones who have trouble keeping up
The ones who have no desire to follow.

I will help the injured and the forgotten,
The elders and the children
And support the seekers who have lost their way.

Our future is not in the vanguard of pride
But in the midst of need.
Our glory not in conquest but in kindness.

LET ME LINGER

It may be a product of getting older
But sometimes I want to stop time.

I want to make the sunsets last just a little longer.
I want the quiet mornings to go on and on

The laughter at the dinner table
To stretch out into a whole evening
The beauty of the clouds as they race
Across the valley to never end.

It is not that I want to freeze reality, just slow it down.
I want life to move as slowly as I do.
For I have learned that life moves far too fast as it is.
It is a joy that endures but briefly
Made of moments that pass as quickly as hummingbirds.

Let me linger in the love I feel.
Let me see the light for as long as I can.

THEY WATCH OVER YOU

They are watching over you,
The ones who have gone before
The ones who know you best,
The spirits of a love that never dies
Your ancestors of hope and courage,
Bright souls who shaped your life
And showed you what life really was.

They watch over you, they hear you and care for you
No matter what comes. No matter what happens
They are there, sheltering you beneath their blessing
Giving you the wisdom you need, the strength you need
To live as they lived, to love as they loved,
To watch in wonder the unfolding of a blanket of dreams.

WHAT WE NEED TO KNOW

Most of what we need to know
We learned on the savannas of Africa
Shortly after we started to walk upright.

We need to know when to run
And when to hold our ground.
We need to know how to understand the signs of change.
We need to know what to eat
And what to avoid to stay healthy.
We need to know how to work together

How to feed the whole community
How to keep our children safe
How to communicate our ideas and our fears.

Life may seem much more complex today
But the same primal wisdom is always within us.
When in doubt, trust your instincts.

LEAVE THE REST TO THE SPIRIT

If I had to express how I believe
In only a very few words
I would say it comes down to this:
I am to take care of the loving
And let the Spirit take care of the judging.

And I like it that way.
I am blessed to be under such a rule.
It frees me from fear. It allows me to listen and learn.
It gives me the grace to let others be who they are
Without the need of my correction.

It keeps me from narrow-mindedness
And pinched self-assurance.
It opens my heart. My work is compassion
Kindness and healing without exception.
I leave the rest to the Spirit who made us all.

LITTLE TO SAY

My ancestors valued silence.
That is the room where the mind goes to think.

The elders say it is not possible
For people to make good choices
If everyone is constantly talking.

Wisdom is not measured by volume.
If it takes an hour to get to the point,
The point has already gone.

Religious or political insight
Does not come with a glib tongue
A fast answer, or a sales pitch.

Listen to the person who has little to say
But always something worth hearing when they do.

The Spirit did not need more than a word
To make the light shine.

ELDERS ARE PEOPLE OF THE FUTURE

My culture respects the elders
Not only because of their wisdom
But also because of their determination.

The elders are tough.
They have survived many struggles and many losses.

Now as they look ahead to another generation
They are determined that their sacrifices
Will not have been in vain
That their children's children will not grow up
In a world more broken than the one they sought to repair.

The elders are voices of justice.
They are champions for the earth.
They defend the conscience of the community.

We follow the elders
Because they have a passion for tomorrow.
They are people of the future, not the past.

THE ETERNAL GRANDPARENTS

They are watching over us,
All those who have gone before.
They are our ancestors,
And they have seen enough in their own lives
To know what we are going through.

They have survived economic collapse,
Social unrest, political struggle,
Even great wars that raged for years.
Now from their place of peace
They seek to send their wisdom into our hearts
To guide us to reconciliation,
To show us the mistakes before we make them.

Their love for us is strong. Their faith in us is certain.
When times get hard, sit quietly and open your spirit
To the eternal grandparents
Who are still a part of your spiritual world.
Receive their blessing, for their light will lead you home.

A BLESSING BARN

Before the coming of the Europeans
My people had a way to prevent poverty in our nation:
Communal barns.
Surplus crops and dried meats were placed
In barns located around the nation.
Anyone could go there and take what they needed.

In this way, no one ever went hungry.

I would like to adapt this idea to blessings.
Some of us may feel we have blessings in abundance.
If so, channel that surplus toward a communal resource—
A blessing barn—
And if any among us may need some extra blessings
Please feel free to draw on this source
In prayer to help you.

Let no one feel hungry for hope
When we have more than enough to share.

NIGHT JOURNEY

It happened again last night
Just as the elders said it would
The quiet voice that speaks when we sleep
To answer our prayers, to show us the way.

It came like whispers, whispers in my dreams
Calling out images from the air,
The first hints of understanding
A vision emerging from behind the clouds.

Did I understand it all? Was the wisdom received?
No, not yet, but keep listening, the elders say
Keep listening, because the Spirit speaks in our dreams

To each and every one,
A night journey made without moving
A message from within,
Given gladly by a love that watches over us
Each of us, through even the longest night.

MY STRENGTH IS IN MY FAITH

My strength is in my faith:
I will not waver in my trust
That whatever may come
In the end the Spirit of goodness and mercy
Will be waiting for me on the other side.

My strength is in my faith:
I will not be resigned to the idea
That a pale approximation of freedom
Is all that we can hope for
But insist that justice alone
Is our future as a diverse family.

My strength is in my faith:
I will not surrender to any illness,
Even those that may take my life
But continue to believe our tomorrow is eternal.

My strength is in my faith:
I will not bend my knee to despair
But love and love always,
Even if the stars should desert the sky
And the earth hide her beauty from the sun

Still I will love and love always
Until my love is so much a part of my life
That I can no longer tell where one ends
And the other begins.

ANCESTORS' BLESSING

Last night I thought I heard the drum
Sounding far away like distant thunder
But steady as a heartbeat
The heartbeat we have danced to for generations.

Hearing that drumbeat made me feel better.
I knew that it must mean my ancestors
Are dancing in heaven
Dancing the old dances that have bound my people together
Since time began.

They are trying to help us just when our need is greatest.
And if they are dancing,
Then the grace they are sending us has begun falling
Falling all around us, falling like starlight, drifting down
To give us strength, wisdom, and hope.

And although I do not know the tradition of the people
Who have gone before you in your culture
I am sure they are dancing for us too
In their own way, but with the same intention
The intention of all of our ancestors in these hard days:

To give us their blessing.

LONG MEMORY

My people are from an oral tradition
Meaning we did not write things down
But told stories or sang songs
To express our history and theology.

Consequently, we are a people with a long memory,
A very long memory.

We did not leave our past behind
But brought it with us
Encoded over generations
In a thousand stories
Kept sacred in ancient songs
Sung beneath the moon.

We know the long thread of hope
That runs through time
Reappearing over and over again
Just when it is needed the most.

Come gather by the firelight.
Come gather on holy ground.
There are many stories we need to share
Many songs we need to sing
Here beneath the moon.

TRAIL OF TEARS

When my ancestors walked the Trail of Tears,
They knew their world was changing forever.
What had been was disappearing and could not return.

What was ahead of them was uncertain.
Many families lost loved ones along the way.
Illness was always a danger,
Especially for the very young and the very old.

There was no magic cure for them,
No government they could trust in their time of need.
All they had was each other and their faith in a Spirit
Who would never abandon them.

Faith got them through. Prayer got them through.
They walked in dignity and hope because they believed.
They survived because they knew the Spirit was with them.

We honor them as a nation that refused to give up
And as a people who showed us
What community really means.
May their memory live long among us
And may we learn from them
What we need in this time for our own long journey.

OKLA TALOA

My people love to sing.
So much so that sometimes you can hear them
Before you see them.

Driving the back roads
Through the mountains in the warm months
Heading for a rural church or campground,
You can turn onto the red dirt trail
And pass beneath the sheltering trees.
Then the sound finds you: the sound of voices
Singing the old songs in the old language.
Okla taloa: the people sing.

Their simple harmony passes
Through the shadow-dappled valleys
And climbs to the top of the highest peak.
It fills the earth and rises into the sunlit sky.
Then you know you are not far from home.

So when times get hard
And you feel the fatigue of these long days
Stop and listen. Listen for the singing. It will find you

Even in the shadows,
Even before you see your way forward.
Let it be your comfort and your guide.
Let it be your blessing. Okla taloa.

VISION

My ancestors said that the Spirit gave
Every creature on earth a special gift.
Bears have great strength
Eagles can soar to great heights
Deer can run at great speed through the forest.

And what about us? What about human beings—
What is our gift?
Vision, the ancestors said: the ability to see
Both what is now and what is coming to be.

We can see the future and adapt to it: that is our gift.
The tribe of the human beings survives
Because we adapt to change.
We do not have to fear the future.
We only have to adapt to it to live in safety.

Thanks to the Spirit for our gift, for our skill,
And for our hope during these days
When our gifts can mean so much.

HEIRLOOM

Your song will not end.
The kindness you have shown.
The wisdom you have shared.
The love you have given. None of that will end.

It will go on and on, passed like an heirloom of faith
From person to person
Not only of your own family,
But between the countless others you have known
Cared for, worked with, prayed for, and respected.

You have made music with your life.
You have made a witness.
The harmony you have embodied
And the hope you have embraced
Will sing on after you,
Sing on into generations yet to come.

Your vision will live in many hearts until one joyous day
It joins the chorus of life that began
When the Spirit first started to sing.

A BELIEVER IN US

Let me make my witness as simply as I can:
I am a believer in second chances
In peace and reconciliation

Because I stand in need of mercy
Knowing life can begin again if love is allowed to heal.
I am a believer in something greater than myself

Greater than all that is, the source of creation
As far as the eye can see, each life and soul cherished
Every innocence redeemed.

I am a believer in kindness and fairness
Because they are words of transformation
Cornerstones of community

The justice we seek right under our noses.
I am a believer in us
In you and me and all the people we have never met
But always knew: the human family we could be
If only we have the courage of our convictions.

MY FATHER'S STORIES

Today the leader of my nation, the Miko,
Came to see my father.
Four other leaders, men and women, came with him.
They came to listen to my father's stories.
My father will turn ninety-nine when the snow flies
So he has many stories to share.

Stories about what it was like
To be Choctaw in the Great Depression.
Stories about his experiences in World War II
Now that he is the last man
Left of hundreds in his company.

The Miko wanted to hear about who he knew,
What he saw, how he felt.
He wanted to time travel with my father
Gliding down the river of his memory
Taking in his memories like food for the soul.

I sat and listened.
Not only to the stories but to the sound of the ancestors
Who were crowding into that small space.
Stories like that draw the spirits of our people

Like wood fire on a cold night.
It is a wise leader, I thought,
Who takes time to listen to stories.

WORDS WILL PASS AWAY

My words will not last,
No matter how wise they may seem
For time will dust them away,
In its endless task of cleaning.

But if by grace I am able to inspire
One other soul to love
To take the risk of love, for the sake of love
Then I will have written something
That will forever endure
For it will be written on the heart
Of another human being.

And though, one day, we will both step
Through the dust of time
And escape its ceaseless cycle
Still our message will live and live and live again
For the reach of love is infinite,
And the life of love is infinite.

Words will one day pass away
But the love we release into creation will never be lost
For through it we are drawn to its source
A place more wondrous than any word will ever convey.

TWO THINGS

Here are two pieces of spiritual information
From the collected wisdom of Native America
That may be helpful for you to know:

(1) There is a Creator who is conscious of
And involved in your life.
(2) This Creator has a sense of humor.

Let those two thoughts just abide
In your heart and mind for a moment.
Do you see the good news here? Do you sense the relief?
These two points alone are reason for us to smile.
The Spirit knows us and accepts us as we are,
No frowns involved.
So take a breath. It is going to be okay.

MYSTIC OF THE ALL-NIGHT DINER

I am the mystic of the dollar store
And the all-night diner.
I am the prophet waiting in the drive-through
To get my coffee.

What is most sacred is usually right in front of us,
Right where we live.
The holy is in the everyday, the common, the simple.
It is hidden in places that have become so routine for us
That we hardly notice them anymore.

There are revelations in the hallway
And epiphanies on the playground.
All around us the Spirit is present
Vibrant and alive,
Just waiting for us to make a connection.
Our spiritual discoveries may sometimes
Be on mountaintops
But nine times out of ten they are made
While looking at old photos
Or hearing a piece of music that suddenly
Makes you a time traveler.

I am the pilgrim of the neighborhood,
The sage of shared wisdom
Stopping by to wish you well,
Bringing you a word you have known all of your life.

THE PATH WORN SMOOTH

If you are walking a long and difficult path
You may find it worn smooth by the number of others
Who have had to pass this way before.

Sorrow and struggle are not new to our human family.
The number of people who have carried heavy loads
Along this same road are too many to count.

You can see the evidence of their passing.
You can also feel their presence
For in their heavy burden
They made their imprint upon the earth.
You can feel them watching over you
Encouraging you to take the next step.

The silent witnesses to our pain walk beside us.
The ancestors of our journey
Lead us to the high ground of hope.
Keep going.

MUCH TO DO

Time to begin again this good work
We have been sent to do.
To feed the hungry, heal the sick, care for the poor.
All of these tasks and a thousand more stand before us.

Peace still beckons across the war-torn countryside
And justice waits to be fulfilled
In the streets of our cities.
Even the earth speaks its own lament
To all who will listen.
We have much to do.

Time then to take a breath, roll up our sleeves
Put aside personal disagreements and get busy.
We can debate our faith in the evening over coffee.
Now is the time for all of us
To be out in the fields of change.

LET THE HEALERS COME FORWARD

In my language healers are called the alikchi.
It is in their honor that I write these words:
Let the alikchi come forward.
Let the healers come forward.

We need them now and in so many ways.
Let them come forward to lead
Our steps to health and harmony.

Healers of every kind.
Healers of the body, healers of the mind.
Healers of the heart, healers of the soul.
Physical healers and spiritual healers.
Healers of conflict and division.
Healers of anger and fear.

Let them all come forward, for I know they are here.
The alikchi are here. I know they are all around us.
They know their gifts. They know what they can do.
Let them come forward, Spirit,
And bless each one as they do.
Empower them to empower us,
That your people may be whole.

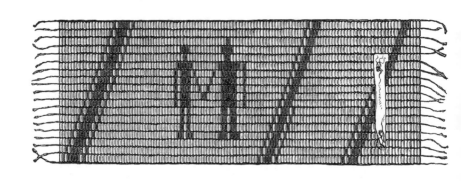

II
KINSHIP
WITH CREATION

IN THE MIDST OF CREATION'S WHEEL

It was not my hand
That sketched the deep valleys of the earth
Or shaped the jagged edges
Of the great mountain's summit.
I did not cast the embers of stars against the night sky
Or pour the waters of the sea onto the dry land.

There is a mind far greater than mine at work
A will and a purpose exceeding what I could even dream.
When life seems out of control, I go outside
To remind myself of that fact.

I stand in the midst of creation's wheel
And watch in wonder the quiet majesty of its turning.
We are in the care of a love without limit or definition
Under the protection of a love that never looks away.

ALL MY RELATIONS

I stand within the circle of life,
Above me the open sky, below me the ground of love.

In four directions I recognize the compass
That binds me to all living things.
This is my spiritual gyroscope:
The equilibrium of kinship.

I walk in balance. I walk in beauty.
I walk the seeker's way.
I listen to the voice of my elders.
I am family before I am me.

I measure what I receive by what I give.
This is the Red Road, ancient and profound,
That leads to the Spirit's good medicine
To the camp of all my relations, the home of every tribe.

SOMEONE WAITED FOR ME

I will not turn for home until I know
We leave no one behind.

I will go and search again, seeking any straggler
Who might not have kept the pace
Any elder who moves a little more slowly
Any person with a burden that weighs them down.

I will seek some sign of them in the shadows.
I will wait beside the road with a light
To guide them to me.
I will not care who they are, where they are from,
Or how they believe:
I will wait to make certain they are safely home
Before the darkness can overtake them.

I will do this because I remember, long ago,
When I struggled to keep up
Someone waited for me. Compassion begins in a memory.

A WILDER SHORE

Come stand with me on a wilder shore
Where age is no impediment to dreams
And life begins anew each dawn
When the Spirit whispers in your ear.

We are not bound by illness
Or chained to time
But live with such a future in our hearts.
Jealous death cannot contain it
Even if one day death will try.

A SINGLE GRACE

O Spirit, alone in your high heaven
Do you ever feel lonely like me?
If you do, then hear my prayer

For all who watch from windows
Waiting beside phones that never ring.
Unloved teens, adults left longing
Elders sitting alone in rooms.

For all citizens of the Big Empty
I ask a single grace.

Let them be discovered today
Like the fine jewel they are
The treasure of someone's heart
Wished from a smaller star.

BLESS THE SEEKERS

Bless the seekers: our traveling tribe
Our motley crew
Caravan of the conflicted and courageous
Stumbling toward paradise

The hurt and the hopeful
Wounded healers
Singing along the way.
Spirit, bless the seekers.

Life within their tents is never easy
But life without them
Would be darkness beyond imagining.

Bless the seekers, dear Spirit, your quarreling brood
Your stubborn flock
Your love living for love
Your dream of what might be.

TO ALL WHO ARE ON THE FRINGE

I would like to say a brief word
In support of the lunatic fringe.

I have been a card-carrying "fringer"
For quite some time now
Out here on the margins of polite society
Where the really interesting people hang out.

I have met wild-eyed dreamers, optimistic visionaries
Unrepentant seekers, and more than a few average folks
Who just like to think for themselves.

Out here there are no party lines to follow
No castes or outcasts, no gated communities of the heart.
There are only envelopes to be pushed,
Barriers to be broken, and love to be risked.

I just want to say to all my fellow fringers:
I am glad to have you out here with me.

NO STRANGERS

There are no strangers.
In the house of the Spirit there are no empty chairs.

All who seek shelter are welcomed.
All who are hungry are fed.
No one is turned away, no one questioned
No one made to wait.

Love is offered freely to any, to every, to all.
Diversity abounds in this household
A tribe of many clans.
Every language spoken, every family at home.

If we are not all here
None of us have arrived.

THE NIGHT SHIFT

I will take the night shift of your prayer
I will keep watch while you sleep
I will be the light glowing in your darkness
The quiet harbor of your dreams.

Be at peace. Be not afraid. All will be well.
Though we pass this night in mystery
Offering the last soliloquy of our lives
We know beyond all doubt
We will face the dawn together.

Rest now.
I have the night shift of your prayer.

HOW SMALL THE WORLD

How small the world is, how very small.
I could reach out to touch Africa.
I could walk across the street to Asia
Around the corner to Brazil.

This earth is a tiny island floating on stardust streams.
It is not the center of all that is
Though people may pretend it so.
It is only a little place, a back garden in need of care.

Intimacy begins in imagination
Compassion in recognition.
How small the distance from my heart to yours.
How near the sound of your breathing.

WE HAVE PASSED THIS WAY BEFORE

We are all travelers
Exploring the span of our lives
As though it was a foreign land
Both origin and destination.

Like all travelers, we find the journey
Sometimes tedious, irritating, and uncomfortable.
Too many strangers, too many crowds
Waiting in lines,
Queuing up to see the same tired wonders.

But then the unexpected happens
The flash of new awakening
The odd feeling we have passed this way before.

We are only tourists in our own time
Until we open our eyes
To find the home we left behind
A landscape undiscovered.

OUR SIBLINGS

All my relatives.
Every living creature
Every bird that flies
Every fish that swims
Every animal that walks the earth:
They are all my relatives.

In the great family of Spirit
The spirals of kinship
Weave us all into relationship
Mutual, caring, connected.

Since all that Spirit does is done in love
All that Spirit created was created in love.
There are no orphans left standing alone
For all are embraced by the compassion
Of a common Creator.

How well we treat our siblings
Is how well we honor our Maker.

THE CIRCLE

Last night beneath the moon
Within the circle of many tribes
The drum sounding like a heartbeat

My family by my side
I knew what it meant to belong.
This is my story.
These are my companions
On a path walked by my ancestors
Of the same spirit.

I pray that all who read these words
Will be blessed by belonging.

May you belong to your own story.
May you find your place by birth or adoption.
May you know your ancestors
And may they know you.

May you be embraced by family
In the circle of those who know you best.

PRAYER AND LAUGHTER

Sometimes I laugh when I pray. I hope you do too.

So often prayer is such a serious business
With so many deep needs and heartfelt petitions
But there are those moments, those rare and happy times
When the thanksgivings start to flow
Like a mountain stream rushing over rocks
Life running through sunlight.

And I cannot help but smile
Smile at the beauty of it all, smile at grace so abundant.

May the Spirit give you reason to laugh today.
May your prayers turn to delight.
May your thanks be said with a smile.
May your life run through sunlight
Prayer and laughter the same.

HOW BEAUTIFUL OUR MOTHER

The earth puts on her white coat, her winter coat
And drapes the rivers, scarves of blue
Around her neck to ward off the chill

The cold air of silent space, as she dances
Always dances, turning and turning again
To spin out the long seasons of her life.

How beautiful she is in her dance
How beautiful our mother, the earth
And how worthy of our love and care.

May she dance forever, twirl and turn
Among the far-flung stars.
And may we never cease to honor her
As she spins and spins beneath the moon.

A TRUST FUND

Whatever I have, I gladly will give to you
And I am a person of great wealth.

I have vast stores of kindness that I can never use up
Great quantities of compassion
Piled to the rafters of my heart
And more love than could fill an ocean many times over.

I have an endless supply of listening.
I have an abundance of patient prayer
A trust fund of trust, huge investments in hope.

We may sit and wonder how we will pay the bills
But we will be rich in what matters.
Come spend your joy with me.
Let us be extravagant in our generosity.

YOU ARE A LIGHT OTHERS CAN SEE

Let me honor you today with the respect you deserve.
Let me acknowledge you as a person
Who has worth and value.

Our world would be diminished without you.
Our journey would seem longer.
You bless us with your presence.
You make a difference in our lives.
We need you.

There are many who would stand to say this with me.
You are loved.
I know you well enough to understand
That you do not expect
Or even want to hear this kind of praise.
But I believe the Spirit intends every human heart
To hear a simple truth: you are a light others can see.

PRAYERS OF A SLEEPING WORLD

In these early hours
When all the world around me is sleeping
I close my eyes and imagine it is so quiet
I can hear the whispered prayers of other souls

Prayers being lifted up around the sleeping world
Prayers from places I will never see
Whispered by people I will never meet
In languages I cannot speak
But with words I already know by heart.

When we pray we are never alone.
We are an unseen family
A community vast and loving
Whispering hope into the quiet
Of a still sleeping world.

NO PRIVATE HEAVEN

My problem with the idea of heaven as a gated community
That only some people will be allowed to enter is memory.

Even if I got to be one of the chosen few
I would not enjoy being in heaven
Because I would remember
All the good people I knew who didn't make it.

I would miss them.
I would worry about them.
I would want to help them.

So the private heaven idea just doesn't work for me.
I know, admire, and respect too many people
From too many different walks of life
To let that life end in anything but love and community.

IF YOU ARE A SEEKER

Sometimes on the spiritual path
It is more fun to walk beside a seeker than a true believer.

I have no quarrel with those who are certain they know
Exactly where they are going on the path of faith
But often their questions are few and their stories familiar.

It is when you listen to the seeker's vision
That things can come alive.
Questions and doubts, longings and hopes
Experiences both difficult and transcendent:
It sounds very honest to me.
And very human.

If you are a seeker, I will be proud to walk beside you
Discovering life as we go.

BEFORE THE CANDLE GOES OUT

The candle burns low.
I have said all the prayers I can say.
I wait in the silence to hear any word returning
From the far side of what I know.

Outside the wind wraps a cold arm around the moon
And the trees wave their empty hands
In surrender to the season.

We each find our own way to the borders of the sacred.
We each learn to listen.
There is no religion when we are alone
Just the wonder of a longing heart
The intimate wait when all the prayers are done.

May you discover what you seek.
May you hear an answer on the wind.
May love find you before the candle goes out.

OUR COMMON SPIRIT

Let us dare to love one another
All of us, no matter how different we may be
No matter how stern the rules
That forbid us to appear in public together.

Let us climb over the high walls of our own doctrine
Sneak past the guards of the caste systems
That tell us we are never to speak to those people
And see what it feels like to be out under the open sky.

For too long our religious fences and racial fears
Have kept us hidden.
Now is the moment for our peaceful insurrection.
Let us dare to love one another
To listen, to learn, to be the friends
Our common spirit tells us we are and always were.

PRAYING

I am praying where I am. You are praying where you are.
Around us millions are praying
In their own places and their own times.

I am praying in my language, you in yours
And together with many others
Our sacred words rise to heaven
In a thousand dialects of the human voice.

I am dreaming my holy dreams. You are dreaming.
The whole world is dreaming
Spinning out hope like a ribbon caught on the morning air.

The Spirit is watching over me.
The Spirit is watching over you.
The Spirit is watching over every soul
Beneath the stars we share.

LET US WALK

Come let us walk, all of us together,
The path of days before us
United in our diversity, free in our spirits,
Confident in the justice of love
Finding peace in every step.

We are, even if we do not know it, a movement, a witness,
A presence of hope in the world around us

For every time people set aside their disagreements
And stand up to be a community not a herd
The ancestors on high rejoice, the poor look up and rejoice.
The lands burnt dry with war
Flow again with springs of life
And the elders watch the horizon
For the day they always dreamed.

Come let us walk, all of us together, until our cause is won.

HANDPRINTS OF OUR HEART

We are all called, each in our own way,
To do the work of creation
Knitting together the many strands of grace
That hold the universe together.

We each have a task to perform,
Even if we are not always aware
Of its true purpose or intent.
We may not even know what good we have done
Until the great cycles of love turn round
And we discover the blessing we have been.

When the curtain parts, we suddenly feel
The cool air of heaven billowing about us
And for only an instant
We know that we have made a difference.

We are all called, called to be what no other can be
The handprint of our heart on the long walls of time.

OUR VOCATION

I believe we are here for a reason.
I believe we were not born into this generation by accident.
I believe that the community of which we are a part
Came into being with a purpose.

In a time when so many shadows hang over our world
Our task is to be an alternative of light.

Where there is doubt, we can inspire hope.
Where there is anger, we can offer reconciliation.
Where there is prejudice, we can embody shared respect.

To do this, we do not have to agree
On how we pray or how we vote.
We only need to agree that what unites us
Is stronger than what divides us:
Our vocation is to show the world that love
Is stronger than fear.

CARD-CARRYING HUMAN BEING

I am a card-carrying human being.
I am not a political party, a denomination,
A class, a race, or a demographic.
I am just a human being.

I am not a nationality, a sexuality,
An age, or even a gender
Since we all start out pretty much the same
And we are all going to the same destination.

I like to do what human beings like to do:
Live at peace, enjoy my life, be with the family.
I like learning from other human beings,
Sharing my own thoughts
And finding ways to make this world safer, happier,
And as natural as we found it.

I am a card-carrying human being.
That means I am proud to be what Spirit made me.

I HONOR YOU

I honor you. I honor you for who you are
And for what you have done.

You did not become the person you are without effort.
You have weathered many storms and seen many changes.
You have kept going when others might have given up.

You have lived your life like an art,
Creating what you did not have,
Dreaming what you could not see.
And in so doing, you have touched many other lives.

You have brought your share of goodness into the world.
You have helped more than one person
When they needed you.

I honor you, for walking with integrity,
For making hope real,
For being who you have become,
I honor you.

I WILL PRAY FOR YOU

I will pray for you in the quiet hours
When only the last stubborn stars
Cling to the brightening sky.

I will pray for you in the small spaces of a busy day.
I will pray for you as I walk beneath the trees
Through city parks where elders feed the birds.

I will pray for you beside a winter window
Looking out to see the snow fall silently
On the sleeping earth.
I will pray for you today and tomorrow

And on the far side of as many years
As the Spirit may grant me.
I will be constant in my prayers
Gently plying my trade of prayer for you
Knowing you are praying for me too.

EVERY POINT ON THE COMPASS

I am grateful for what I have learned
From people of different faiths.
I am proud to have friends
From every point on the compass of religion.

In listening to their words I have heard a different story
One that challenges me to think on ever deeper levels.

In trying to see creation through their eyes
I have captured visions of the complexity
Of our spiritual reality.

They have made me uncomfortable,
And for that I am truly thankful
For complacency and arrogance
Are sure signs of the smug soul.
I share what I believe and respect others who do the same.

SPIRIT OF ALL

If we are all created in the image of the Spirit
Then how wonderfully diverse the Spirit must be.

The Spirit in every shape and size
The Spirit in every tone and color
The Spirit in every face and body.
The Spirit of all cultures and languages
Of all peoples and nations
Of all ages and genders.

When we cease to see the Spirit
Through the keyhole of our own comfort
And witness the grandeur of the Spirit
Without limits or definitions
Then the image becomes infinite
And the subject becomes intimate.

We do not need to think outside the box
Because there is no need for the box at all.

COMMON CAUSE

The more things in this world seem to slide out of control
The more we need every person
Of every faith and every tradition
To stand together to hold the center of love.

Now is not the time for us to hang our heads in despair
But rather to raise our expectation
Of what a united community can do
When it has the will to do it.

Across all lines of imagined division,
Against all odds of reaction
We extend our hands and hearts
To every person around our Mother Earth
Who will join in the struggle
For peace, reconciliation, and justice.
Faith is not a sign of our difference
But a clear call to our common cause.

NIGHT PRAYERS

Night is drawing near. Soon the night prayers will begin.
The after-hours prayers.
The prayers without the need for words.
Spoken from the heart.
The language of those who work the late shift of sorrow.

Night prayers turn bar rooms into churches,
Motels into temples, truck stops into shrines.
Night prayers are first-time prayers,
Last-chance prayers, prayers tossed up into the stars
To see if anyone is there to catch them.
Prayers without expectation.

Tonight I will pray with the midnight seekers
And the far-from-home angels.
I will offer my own night prayer.
For them. With them.
In the congregation of the all-night diner.

BORN KNOWING

I think we know. I think we are born knowing.
Somewhere inside, in our souls,
We have this instinctive awareness
That we are the children of a caring presence.

Over the years we may learn
To call this presence by many names.
We may define our feelings
In the language of faith and dogma.
We may even let the instinct go and walk away
Thinking we were wrong all along.

But I believe we know
Because no matter what we do, the love never leaves us.
You and I are loved, loved by a common parent
Loved all of our lives, loved until we pass over
To discover the truth in the heart of a child.

ALL LIFE IS ONE

I had a living reminder of kinship the other day.

I was with a small circle of friends.
We have known each other for years.
We are from different Native American nations.
We are an aging group of activists
Who have fought many battles
For the causes we believe in.

What has held us together is kinship.
We care for one another.
We see our differences as our strength.
We understand that what happens to one happens to all.
We have faith in the first creed
The one humanity knew before language:

All life is one, all creation is one, all time is one.
Kinship is celebrating the one within the many.

OUR LINE IN THE SAND

Justice for the poor is not negotiable.
Protection and care for children and elders
Is not one option among many.
Compassion for the sick and suffering is not expendable.
Peace is not the default position
If power doesn't get us what we want.

The line drawn in the sand by faith is clear.
Whatever tradition we may choose to follow
The spiritual path leads us all to the same side of that line.
We must make our stand for what we believe:

That every human being deserves to be treated with dignity
And every living thing with respect.
Our line in the sand is clear.
Love compromised is faith denied.

SIBLINGS IN SORROW

I have watched my hopes fall like china cups to the floor.
I have swept up the pieces and gone back to start again.

No spiritual life is without pain.
No human heart has remained unbroken.

Here, then, is a word to any who are in a time of challenge:
Do not despair.
You have many praying for you with understanding.

They are your siblings in sorrow. They have felt it too.
We survive not through strength but through sharing.

TRUST INSTEAD THE SEEKER

I have lost my way more times than I can remember.
I have taken wrong turns, made long detours
Found myself at a crossroads
With no clue which way to go.

When it comes to walking the spiritual path
It is not always wise to follow the directions
Of someone who claims to never be wrong.

Trust instead the fellow seeker
Who admits to the reality of ambiguity
Who understands the terrain of doubt
Who knows the persistence of a heart
That longs for love and always will.

Be guided not by certainty but by honesty.

WE WILL NOT STOP

We will not give up, go away, or be quiet.

We will remain here
Standing in the way of the victory parade
Spoiling the photo op
Embarrassing the guests at the penthouse party.

We will continue to resist repression.
We will not allow a return to a culture of closets.
We will not pretend there is no threat to the earth.
We do not think we have all the answers
But we will never stop asking the questions.

We are the quiet people of the center
The struggling people of the margins
The survivors from the bottom rung.
We are the new community of faith
Unified by a shared vision of human dignity
Strengthened by a belief in the power of love.

Until history moves toward justice
We will not give up, go away, or be quiet.

KINSHIP

Here is a simple but profound piece of wisdom
From the tradition of America's Indigenous people:
Kinship is the spiritual cornerstone for community.

Kinship is the sense of relatedness
The acknowledgment that all of life is interconnected
And mutually dependent.

Kinship bonds humanity to creation
And unifies diversity into a matrix of compassion.
It says we need one another and must care for one another
No matter how different we may seem.

Kinship is the basis for an ethical society.
Power builds on fear. Kinship builds on trust.

I SEE YOU THERE

I see you there. Standing on the edge of the crowd.
Standing alone quietly in the noise and confusion.

You look like an island,
A small island in the midst of a restless sea.
You are here with the others
But somehow not a part of them.

Your eyes are fixed elsewhere, somewhere far away
Somewhere only you can see.

The crowd cannot contain you.
Your vision has set you apart.

You are only one among the many
But you are the one who can see clearly.

You have that gift and that burden.
I see you there and I know that you can see me.

NOTE TO A SPIRITUAL SKEPTIC

I am asking you to join me on this journey
Not because I want to convert you to anything.

I have no rules for you to follow if you come along
No promises of eternal rewards
Or threats of eternal punishments.
To be honest, I don't even have a real idea
Of where we are going.

In many ways, it is all a great mystery.
And that's why I need you:
To help me understand it, to question it,
To discover what's really out there.

The "it" is what I believe is the source of all life
And searching for that source is what I call faith.
So please think about my invitation.
I don't want to convert you. I want to amaze you.

DANCING THROUGH THE DARK HOURS

Let us dance through these dark hours
While others crouch down
Seeking shelter from a worried world
Hiding in the shadows
Afraid to hope for tomorrow.

Let us give them a sign they can see
A message made of music and motion
Two dancers spinning light out of darkness
A waltz in an air raid shelter
Unafraid, unbound, unleashed from this earth
Rising with every step, a dance to lift the human soul.

Let us dance so others can dance
Dancers from every direction
Standing up to join us
Music filling the sky
A revolution of unrestrained joy

An invitation to believe again, to hope again
To be free again, dancing through these dark hours
As if dancing were all that we were born to do.

COME STAND HERE

All of you who are frightened and confused,
Come stand here.

Here on the high ground of reason
Here on the rock of faith unshaken
Here where you can see tomorrow

Without the hype and the spin.
Come stand here, for there is room for everyone.
Room for people of every color and culture
Of every memory and story.

Come stand here, in the midst of the madness
Here where others can see us and take hope.
Do not be afraid
But believe in the foundation beneath us:

Justice and mercy, truth and integrity
Common sense and compassion.
We may have moved from them
But they have not moved from us.

Come stand here, in freedom and love
And together we will build the sanctuary
For which so many have longed and so many have prayed.

KEEPERS OF MYSTERIES

I will not forget you. Don't worry about that.
We have been through too much together
For either of us to forget.

We carry the same message into the world:
Hope when hope seems fragile.
Courage when courage is needed.
Faith in what we cannot see until we do.

We are keepers of many mysteries:
How the human heart endures, why love never grows old
Where to find the wild places when you need them.
We learned all of this together. How could I forget?

How could any of us forget?
The blessing was already received, long before we met.

I WILL NOT STOP CARING

I will not stop caring, whatever the cost.
I will not cease loving, no matter the consequences.

The political winds may howl above me
Scattering people like leaves in a storm
But I will hold fast to the common ground
The wisdom that once formed us.

Difference is not a crime.
Diversity is not a threat.
Disagreement is not a failure.

Community requires of me what it requires of others:
A commitment to share in the process of justice.

There are no expendable human beings in that process
Only a sacrifice of privilege.
For the sake of the many,
I will not stop caring for the few.

HOW TO HELP

Want to help? Here's how:
Help your elders by listening
Help your children with the gift of your time
Help your spouse with patience

Help your friends with understanding
Help your worship place with a pledge
Help your coworkers with cheerfulness
Help your community by volunteering

Help the hungry with food
Help the homeless with shelter
Help the earth with commitment
Help the guilty with reconciliation

Help the hurting with prayer
Help the Spirit with your energy
Help the enclosed with a visit
Help the addict with courage

Help the bereaved with comfort
Help yourself with the help of the Spirit.

LOVE THE ONES WHO FOLLOW

I celebrate the wisdom that binds us together
The collective memory of our ancestors
The ancient vision that takes a new shape
With each passing generation.

We are not random seekers searching blindly
For some message of meaning.
We are scouts with a mission.
We have been sent out for a purpose.

Each one of us was given a medicine bag
A star to follow, and a new name.
We take it from there, traveling with the Spirit
To valleys we have never seen
Beneath mountains we cannot name.

Guided by a compass of the heart
And a map drawn in pictures:
We have found our way.
We have broken a trail for others to follow.

So do not doubt the gift you have given
But honor the ones who showed you the way
And love the ones who will follow.

THE SPIRIT WHO STAYS LATE

My life is not the serene spirituality
Of quiet contemplation.
I do not live the saintly life,
Far removed from mundane matters

But dwell down here with the dirty dishes and diapers.
With monthly bills, sneezing kids,
And an old car that runs on prayer.

I do laundry. I clean toilets. Not the stuff of legend.
I need help in my chore-filled life,
Grace my routine to renew
The Spirit who always stays late
To help on the clean-up crew.

AT HOME

I want you to feel at home.

If I try to describe what impact
I want my words to have on those who read them
This is one way to express it:

I want you to feel so welcomed to this place
So intertwined with all those you see around you
So comfortable in expressing yourself
That you would call it like being at home.

The deepest level of kinship we have
Is when we no longer feel like strangers in our own home
But like family in a place meant for us to share.

This is an ancient vision yet to be realized.
The vision of a home.
Relationships balanced into a life
That excludes none and honors all.

Welcome home.

III
VISION OF
THE SPIRIT

TURN THE WHEEL OF TIME

Do I have some knowledge of what is to come?
Can I see into the future? Yes, I can.
Not because I am a prophet or a clairvoyant,
But because I am making that future right now.
By what I choose to do or not do, say or not say,
I am shaping what is to come.
And so are you. So are we all.

We do not need second sight or a crystal ball
But only a sense of personal responsibility.
We are not the observers of history but participants.
As close to home as the love we share,
As far as the most distant village, our choices count.
We make hope happen. We turn the wheel of time.

WAITING FOR THE FIRST WORD

What is one of your best spiritual memories?

One of mine is of sitting in silence
With a group of Navajo elders.
We are on benches in the shade of a brush arbor
Watching the desert sun walk across Monument Valley.

The contrast between light and dark
The burning sand and the cool shadow
Is a physical experience.

The earth before us is beyond age.
The silence we share radiates out into the valley
As if we are waiting for the first word
In all creation to be spoken.

It is from memories in every life
That faith is woven into life
Not from the rules we follow but the visions we remember.

PATTERNS

Please give me the ability to comprehend, Spirit
To see the pattern without missing the detail.

Help me understand the meaning of the complexity
That surrounds me
Not with facile answers but with genuine integrity.

Let me encounter my life.
Let me be mindful of what I have to learn.

With diligence I will strive
To free myself from assumptions.
With joy I will anticipate new discoveries.

Give me a touch of your deep wisdom, Spirit
And I will follow it like a sailor
Looking up to read the stars.

DAY BEGINS

The monk in me likes sacred routine.
Each morning I awake
With the words thank you on my lips.
Each morning I touch the earth
From the center of the Four Directions.
I send my heart flying.
I send it sailing as high into the blue sky as I can.

Whether riding stormy winds
Or catching a ride on lazy clouds
I let the words of my heart go free.
They will speak for me.
They will tell my story, offer my thanks, share my hope.

The ancestors will gather my prayers like flowers.
They will know the sound of my voice.
So before the first thin streams of light
Touch the sleeping horizon
Their blessing will abide with me come what may.

So my day begins.
My life set once more on the course to discovery.
Just like yours.

FLOATING

They say shamans can fly.
I just float.

Out over housetops, drifting on the night wind,
Watching the world sleep.
I hear the prayers of good hearts, rising on currents of hope,
To circle the vesper moon.
I see the angels keep ceaseless rounds,
Night-shift nurses with violet wings
Outspread to shelter those in need.

Be at peace. Rest in peace.
Prayer covers you. Angels guard you. The Spirit loves you.
Float, just float. All through the night.

AN HONOR DANCE

I was in Cheyenne country last night
Gathered around the drum
As the ancient songs rose into the night sky.

I was there with people from many Native nations
Attending an honor dance for a revered elder
My own spiritual mentor of many long years past.

The Great Spirit enfolded us in a shawl of starlight
The sliver of the moon a pale eye sleeping.

All people have a tradition to share.
All cultures have a beauty within them.

I give thanks for our diversity
For the songs we sing, the circle of our proud memory.

A POOL OF WONDER

Come sit with me beside a pool of wonder.
Take time to watch still water.
See how deep your mind can go
When you drop it like a stone
Into hidden depths of the heart
Where even reason cannot follow.

We will never know every answer.
Our task is to be stewards of the mysteries of Spirit
In awe of what we have yet to learn,
Mystics beside the pool of living water
Where shadows are as welcome as the sun.

WHAT DID YOU LEARN?

In the end, it may all come down to a single question:
So what did you learn?

I have no more insight
Into the meaning of life than anyone else
But I have come to trust in my own experience.

I know I am not in charge of this reality.
I know I am not the center of the universe.
I also know that my time here is not by accident.

I am here for a purpose. For a reason.
Beyond the positive imprint of my love that I leave behind
My role in this creation is to learn as much as I can.

To see the patterns and understand their meaning.
To achieve wisdom by embodying humility.

I believe this because I know that one day I will be asked:
So what did you learn?

DOUBT MAY BE A DOOR

I do not ask for the Spirit's presence in my life
Because I am an empty mind waiting for truth.

Faith is not the absence of critical thought
But thought put to the greatest question.

We were made to reason, to wonder, to ask,
For only by these gifts do we discover
The far reaches of the Spirit's imagination.

Religion is not a court but a laboratory.
We were not made to conform but to explore.
Even doubt may be a door.

THE SHADOWS AND THE SNOW

Maybe it's the times in which we live,
Or maybe it's just my age
Or maybe it is the solstice season,
But every year around now
I seem to step over into an alternate reality, a dreamy
Somewhat sad but always beautiful place
Where memories appear and reappear
And figures move just out of focus

While the past covers the present with a mist
Like frost picked up by a passing wind.
I see the old faces, the familiar faces
A name teetering on the edge of my mind
The citizens of a time floating off into mystery.

Maybe it is just an old man's romantic notions
During the short winter days,
Or maybe it is the Spirit
Helping me find my place in the shadows and the snow.

THE SPIRIT LIVES NEXT DOOR

I still have trouble believing the Spirit lives next door.
I thought Spirit lived far away, in a gated community.

But at times I find the Spirit shuffling around next door
Early of a morning, coffee cup in hand
Looking a lot like me.

Spirit waves, I wave
But this neighbor Spirit
Disconcerts me with such nearness.

Until I need a favor.
Then I am glad the Spirit lives nearby
And is always home when needed.

I peep over the fence for a chat
A time to borrow what I need
And never be asked to return it.

I SUSPECT YOU KNEW

I suspect that you knew you were different at an early age.
Not that you stood aloof or failed to find friends
But that you carried an awareness of life
That was not easy to share.

It was not just your outward sign,
How you appeared to others
But an inward reality, a way of seeing,
A sense of something sacred.
And so you held your secret close,
Listening, waiting, until your time came
Until your name was called by a voice familiar.

You are what you were meant to be. You are called.
You have a story that must be lived to be told.
But I suspect you know that.

WILD PLACES

A voice crying in the wilderness.
The call of the Spirit does not come
In the quiet spaces of comfort.

It beckons us from wild places: that interior wilderness
Just outside the walls of polite society

The dark woods where we are afraid
We may meet the stranger.
It is the risky land of encounter.

The invitation of the Spirit is to go out by going in.
To question what we know. To encounter what we fear.

We are purified not with drops of water
But with beads of sweat.

ONLY BY OBSERVATION

I dreamed that all the religions fell silent.

We woke to a world where no priest could preach
No mullah proclaim
No rabbi teach
No guru explain.

Our holy books turned to blank pages.
In matters of faith we could converse
Only by observation.
We could speak of other things
But in matters of belief we were stilled.

The world became a silent witness:
If others do not see Spirit in what you do
They will not hear it in what you say.

THE SECOND LIFE

There is a heaven.
I know this beyond doubting, for I have been there.

There is a second life to come.
I believe this without question, for I have experienced it.

Heaven is when you are where you most want to be
Doing what you want to do with the ones you love.

The second life comes to us in many ways.
After addiction, after cancer, after grief, after betrayal:
There are many afterlives we have survived to live again.

I do not know if I should expect wings and a harp
But I will settle for these heavens and second chances.
And be grateful to the Spirit forever.

MEMORY IS WHO I WILL BE

I sometimes think the only things of value
I have ever been able to make
Are the memories I have created.

They say that when we pass from this life
Memories are all we take with us.

As I grow older I believe it is true,
For I find myself watching many of the things
I thought important diminish and change
While my memories of people and places
Become all the more precious.

I wince at the ones that still bring me pain
But smile to the core of my soul
At the ones that embody love.
Memory is what I have and who I will one day be.

WHAT THE WIND SAYS

Listen to the wind. It has something to tell you.
Whether it is as quiet as the current
That lifts the hawk to circle the sky
Or as loud as the storm chasing high waves to shore:
The wind has something to say.

There is a word for each of us, a message sent directly
That flows through the wind each day
Offering us insight and vision, clarity and creative ideas
If only we will stop long enough to receive it.

Be still. Be awake. Trust your spiritual senses.
Listen to the wind. The Spirit is speaking to you.

I HONOR YOU TODAY

You are a seer in all but name
A woman of visions, a man of dreams
A person who wraps the spiritual around them
Like a blanket of stars

Looking out into the empty places, the small spaces
The forgotten corners of a gray world
To see the colors that still shine through

When sunlight crawls between the concrete
And smiles find their way
Past the grim guards of convention.

You are an instigator of hope, an agent of peace,
A teacher of the fine art of making life up as you go.

I honor you today
Woman of visions, man of dreams.

THESE QUIET WORDS RISE

I sit with the velvet cloak of night
Hung round my shoulders
Watching the candlelight,
Listening to the silent world breathing in dreams.

My prayers rise on the thin stream of heat
Rising from the flame
Rising in whispers that pass between the stars
Rising into the ear of the One who never sleeps.

Mercy, comfort, hope: rising into the night.
Peace, protection, healing: rising into the night.
Work, family, friends: rising into the night.

On and on they rise, these quiet words
Turned to light, even in the deep-dreamed darkness.

SPEECHLESS LOVE

Now more than ever, our world needs
A renewed sense of the transcendent.

We have lost our capacity to feel awe.
Therefore we have lost our humility.

We live in an age that imagines we are in control
Mesmerized by the latest gadgets of our own creation
Assuming all the answers
Will soon be within our utilitarian grasp.

We make money, not dreams.
We look at screens, not the sky.
We are diminished by the delusion of greatness.

I pray a renewal of breathless wonder back into our lives
A return to speechless love before the holy.

I PRAY A QUIET LAKE

I drove around an old lake,
A quiet lake surrounded by tall trees
In a late afternoon
When the sun was drifting toward the horizon
And the dark clouds were gathering
To welcome the night with rain.

I looked across the still water.

I breathed in the sense of peace that was nothing more
Than the natural world
Slowly going about its business of beauty.

Even in the most difficult times, the most hectic times
We are embraced by the endless cycles of life around us.
We are held in the palm of peace, if only we look to see it.

I pray a quiet lake in your life,
The scent of rain in the distance.

THE WILDER SHORES

I know there is more than a little of the mystic within you.

You have lived on the wilder shores of faith
Along the rocky coast of polite religion
Where visions can roll in like storms
And the Spirit can move like a strong wind from the sea.

There is more the scent of woodsmoke
Around you than incense
Something older, something from the earth
A faith that has deeper roots
An ancient memory that remembers the source of wonder.

There is more than a little of the prophet within you
The quiet word of what is coming
The kind word of what it means
The word of wisdom
To spin another dream from the pale light of the moon.

THE WATCHFUL EYE

On cold winter nights
When Mother Earth sleeps soundly
Beneath her blankets of snow
The Spirit walks in silence
Seeking any who have become lost on their way home.

There is no life left unnoticed by the Spirit.
There is no child forgotten, no elder dismissed,
No prisoner unworthy of recognition,
No addict left alone, no lonely soul abandoned.

Even the hidden ones among us
The silent ones who try to bear their burdens unspeaking
Are under the watchful eye of the Spirit.

On even the coldest nights
The Spirit walks the back roads and the city streets
Holding the light of love just a little higher
For those who expect to see only shadow.

PRESENCE

There is one truth to which I can testify
A reality not conjured from theories
But from the hard core of personal experience.
It is this:

In a world that is forever changing
Making life an endless shell game of chance
There is one constant presence
One unmoving, unchanging, personal presence
That abides through all the vagaries
Of our existence.

You can give it a name or not. It is the same.
It is a love that is conscious, aware, caring, feeling
Active in ways both wise and wonderful.

My faith is not arrived at from an intellectual exercise
But rather from a deep experience.
I have encountered this presence
Again and again and again.

FROM ONE STORY TO ANOTHER

Back from a long night on the road
Skimming the early morning highways
Following gray ribbons through rain and fading stars
Driving on the instinct to come home
To return from one story to another.

How often different realities live next door.

In the rural places, far from the clutter of the city
Voices speak over cups of coffee
And clocks are only a suggestion.

In the city, streets hum and honk the urban anthem
Never able to sit still.

We live in layers, passing between the cultures we create
Crossing between worlds we only recognize
When we leave them far behind.

THE SAME POWER

The same power that set the sun aflame
As though it were a candle
The same power that spun the Milky Way like a pinwheel
The same power that sprinkled stars
Like confetti across the distant heavens:

That very power holds you safe
Under the shelter of its eternal care.
The universe is not unconscious. Creation is not unaware.
All that was and is and ever will be
Resides in the mind and purpose of a presence
Beyond our comprehension or control.

That presence is the source of life
Of love, of intricate beauty and sublime serenity.
That presence is with you, today, and will be forever.

WHAT IS HOLY IS NOT TAME

I have seen the Spirit moving behind the gathering clouds
With wings the color of rainbows.

I have watched the light of creation split the sky
As angels pound the drums of heaven.

What is holy is not what is tame
What is divine is as wild as desert rain.

Love is not a timid breeze but a storm of change
Sweeping the comfortable before it like leaves

Blowing the dust off our ordered lives
Challenging us to dare the elements of our own vision.

What is holy is not what is tame
So when you stand to pray, stand facing the wind.

SPIRITS OF CREATION

I looked up, and as if in a dream, I saw them:
Ancient spirits of the earth.

I saw them come from the mesas,
Gliding on rain clouds above the desert
Flashing lightning as they passed.

I saw spirits from the forest,
Rising up to dance on the trees.
I saw mountain spirits trailing snow-white capes of wind,

And I saw the spirits of the sea
Moving like a storm toward the land.
The earth is not barren but alive,
Filled with the spirits of life
The forces of nature around us,
Old powers from the time of beginning.

The Spirit is not constricted to temple walls
But roams the wild places
Attended by spirits of creation.
We have only to look to see them.

BRING THE JOY FORWARD

The great day is coming. I can feel it in my bones.
I can feel it on the wind.
The day when things change for the better,
When the pendulum swings
When something wonderful finally happens.

Like countless generations before me,
I live in a holy expectation.
I believe that goodness will prevail,
That justice will be done,
That peace and mercy will flow
Like a river into the desert.

Call me foolish, call me naive,
But I will keep working hard each day
Keep doing all I can to bring the joy forward,
And keep watching the horizon
For the light I know will come.

LOVE WILL NOT LOSE

Love will not lose.

Even if the evidence of the daily news
Seems to suggest that it will
Even if we despair of the values we thought we shared
Even if we imagine the divisions between us
Have grown too wide:

Love will not lose.

Love cannot be constrained by legal walls
Political pieties or institutional fear.
Love is the subversion of power by mercy.
It is the uncontrolled spirit of hope
That erodes the authority of oppression.

Love is the human soul made visible.
Once we see it in one another's eyes
No force on earth can compel us to deny its reality.
No matter what it takes, no matter how long it takes

Love will not lose.

MIND AND SPIRIT

Spiritual vision is seeing
With mind and heart at the same time.
It is like getting your soul in focus
Balancing what the mind interprets
And the spirit encounters.
It is something we can all do.

Vision is not a trance or a dream but a way of perception.
It begins in childhood when we learn to navigate
A twin world of wonder and facts.
We develop a sense of equilibrium by doing that.

We live briefly in a sacred way
Walking with intellect and imagination in step.
As we grow in the Spirit
We become intentional about seeing clearly.

We have to open our mind and our spirit together.
We have to understand what we cannot know.

IRONY

The more I let go of my life
The more it seems to make sense to me.

The less I try to control
The more things seem to come within my grasp.

The fewer things I own
The more satisfied I seem to feel.

Spirituality is an irony.
It is based on the counterintuitive principle
That less is more
That giving away is gaining
That being able to bend
Is the best way to stand tall.

These lessons are learned by experience
By seeing and listening.
They are not dogma but common sense.
The more I realize I do not know, the more I learn.

MADE FOR FREEDOM

We are not made for resignation.
Passive acceptance is not the code written into our spirit.

If that were true, as a species,
We would have vanished long ago.
For millennia we have shaken off the temptation
To simply accept reality
The demand that we bend the knee.

We have stood up to struggle against the odds
To change the situation, to find an answer and a healing.

Those deep drives are the energy we call hope.
Those active forces are what determine our future.

We are not made for resignation.
We are made for freedom.

ONE OF THOSE DAYS

Some days I feel so discouraged
I am not sure it is worth turning on the news.

This is not one of them.

Some days I doubt
The human family will ever live in peace and respect.

This is not one of them.

Some days I think healing has passed me by.

This is not one of them.

Today I believe in the final victory of hope over fear.
I believe in the worth and dignity of every human being.

Today I believe all will be well with me
Through the love and grace of the Spirit.

I may have bad days again
But this will not be one of them.

Today I choose to stand again as a believer
In the future before me.

Some days I believe I can change the world.
This is one of them.

WORDS RISING

I have seen the prayer flags fluttering,
In the thin and cold mountain air
Bright bits of color against a turquoise sky,
Flags of love and compassion.

I have seen the candles flicker,
In the hushed vaults of cathedrals
Tiny lights in the peaceful darkness,
Signs of longing and gratitude.

I have seen the dancers moving,
Feathers and fringe beneath the moon
Circling the drum that summons them,
Ancient steps retraced a thousand times.

I have seen my own words rising,
Whispered dreams of healing
Rising into stillness like streams of smoke
From a fire that has been burning
Since time and hope began.

SACRED VISIONS

Do not be shy about claiming the visions you have seen.

I know that in our time and culture
It is not as common for people to speak
Of their spiritual visions
But that does not mean the visions themselves
Have ceased to appear.

The Spirit still sends messages to each of us
Images that are unique to our experience
Flashes of meaning for us to interpret and understand.

Some we seek, some come unbidden
But all are authentic parts of a spiritual life.
The sacred is a visual realm. Wisdom is in what we see.

WE CANNOT GO BACK

The time draws near
When those bent by oppression
Will straighten themselves in pride once more
Rise up and claim their long-withheld birthright
And bring the light of justice to a darkened land.

This is not prophecy but history
The lessons of a thousand generations
Who have seen the pendulum swing
From the powerful few who seek to rule
To the many denied the freedom they deserve.

We cannot go back. Diversity is destiny.
Equality our shared vision.
The earth our common care.
No force can bury what lives
Nor silence what speaks
In so many hearts who hold the human spirit sacred.

DIDN'T GET THE MEMO

I guess I didn't get the memo
The one that defines how we are supposed to act
When we get older.

I am not dismayed by how this world has changed
Because it is always changing.

I am not left longing for how things were in my time
Because this is my time.

I have not grown entrenched in my opinions
But broadened my horizons to be more open
Than ever before.

I do not believe I am on the sidelines but in the vanguard
Because elders are always closer to the future.

And I do not feel alone because I walk proudly
Beside so many others of my generation
Who don't seem to have gotten the memo either
Or, if they did, just tossed it in the place where it belongs.

THE WAY TO TOMORROW

If someone asks you why you are such a dreamer
Tell them it's because reality can't keep up with you.

Claim your right to be a visionary,
To see into the future with hope
To imagine what could happen
If the sacred could just tip the scales toward justice.

Don't settle for what is, but reach for what might be.
Let your mind gather the facts
And your heart sort out the reasons
But open your spirit to soar to the realm of possibility.

The bland prophets of the status quo
May think they own today
But it is dreamers like you
Who slip past them to discover the way to tomorrow.

Reality is just a rearview mirror.

LISTEN TO THE LEAVES

When I was a small child
I would listen for the voice of the Spirit in the trees.
The rustling leaves would whisper their messages
But I was not sure I understood them.

Listen some more, my great-grandmother would say
Go out and listen some more
And one day you will understand it.

I have been doing as she said for many decades now.
And while I still have a lot to learn,
One thing I do know for certain:
The wind in the trees knows us by name.
If you don't believe me, go out and listen.
Close your eyes, listen to the leaves,
And hear your name written on the wind.

WHAT I HAVE SEEN

I have seen things I cannot explain,
Mysteries that will stay with me forever.

I have seen patients recover from illnesses
That should have taken them from this life.
I have seen people overcome addictions
That had trapped them for years.

I have seen violent situations become calm
With only a few words spoken in love.
I have seen great leaders emerge from obscurity.

I have seen poor people stand up to power and win.
I have seen acts of reconciliation between people
Who were estranged for years.

I have seen all of this and much more,
The mysteries of the Spirit,
The visible power of the holy
Changing human lives right in front of my eyes.

WHY NOT THIS DAY?

This is the day when things change for the better
When the healing begins
When hope returns like a long-lost friend.

This is the day when peace breaks out
When people start coming to a reasonable compromise
When common sense and the common good
Finally get their chance to be heard.

This is the day when the breakthrough happens
When old hearts become young again
When laughter can be heard once more.

Of all the days when miracles can start to happen
When love can start to grow
When your life can be touched by a great blessing:
Why not now, why not here, why not this day?

PRAYING FOR ME

Somewhere on this crowded planet
In a place I have never been before
And will never visit in my lifetime
Someone I do not know and will never meet
Has just said a prayer
In a language I do not understand
As an expression of faith in a religion I do not accept.

And yet the prayer was for me.

Please bless all those who are in need,
The stranger prayed, and that includes me.
The wonder of faith is not that we all agree,
But that we all care, even when we are strangers.
So I return the prayer: please bless all who are in need.
All, please, not some:
For they are praying for me as I pray for them.

THE LANDSCAPE OF THE SACRED

A park bench not far from where I live
Has a view of the valleys of heaven.
A sidewalk two blocks over
Leads to the shores of the sea of eternity.
A hill not far from here
Rustles with the sound of angel wings
When you walk up it just before nightfall.

The landscape of the sacred is all around us.
The reality of the Spirit dwells next to us
Each and every day, only the blink of an eye away.
Look closer: the passage to an infinite dream
Is as near as your own neighborhood.

SOMETHING ON THE WIND

There is something on the wind.
That's what the elders used to say
When they felt something different coming.

Perhaps it was because they were farming people
Trained to keep an eye on the weather
But this had less to do with crops than it did with change.

They would look out toward the horizon,
Shelter their eyes against the sun,
And then pronounce the homespun prophecy
For any who would listen.

Now, all these years later,
I finally understand what they meant.
There is something on the wind.
Something unseen, but still tangible.
You can sense it. You can feel it.
A new reality suddenly presents itself.

We may not be sure where it came from
Or what it will do now that it is here
But the winds of change have begun to blow.
Things will not be the same again.

TIME TO COME IN

When I was very small and lived on a farm
I had a playground of fields and flowers
That seemed endless.
Rows of corn over my head,
A cave of a barn, dark and cool
The tire swing beneath the ancient elm.
I had no fear but went where I liked
The prince of a poor family
Living in the riches of the earth.

Only one voice could call me back,
My grandmother on the porch
Her long skirt billowing in the breeze
Calling me to come in, for bad weather was coming
And it was time to be inside.

I never questioned how she knew a storm was near
For she always knew.
I ran to be beside her
In the shelter of our farmhouse home.

Now, all these years later, I see her on the porch
Her hand to her eyes, watching the clouds, feeling the air

Then calling out to the world around her:
Time to come in, time to shelter,
Time to watch how the wind is blowing.

FULL MOON

Last night I drove a lonely road through the countryside.
I followed my headlights over the gray ribbon before me
Watching a full moon rise among the windswept clouds
That tried to hide it from my view.

There is hope, I thought.
There is the pale light that shines in the darkness.

Sometimes what we long for is covered by clouds.
Sometimes we feel like we are driving
Alone on an empty road.
Sometimes we just want to get home.

That is when the moon becomes our sign of the Spirit.
No matter how dark the night or winding the road
The light of the Spirit is still watching over us.
It is still there. It is always there.
All we have to do is look up to see it.

HOW THIN THE SPACE

How thin the walls between earth and heaven.
How close the space between us.
A blink. A look away.
In an instant the gap is closed,
The two realities flowing together
Like rivers passing in the moonlight.

If you are still enough in your soul
You can hear the footsteps of your ancestors
Just a breath away.
We are not isolated in a mechanical clock universe
For no rhyme or reason
But fellow citizens of a creation alive with purpose,
Animated by love,
Drawing time forward to disappear in a timeless grace.

On a clear day you can see the angels flying.

CALLED TO GATHER

Last night I dreamed the spirits of the earth
Were being called from all Four Sacred Directions
Called to gather beneath the watchful moon,
Called to dance beneath the stars.

And so they came, from all points of the wind,
From every land and sea
All flying here, to Turtle Island,
To the place of emergence and return.

Somber were their faces, but determined were their voices
As they took up the ancient chants, the oldest chants,
Words of healing older than time.

They were dancing to rescue the earth.
They were dancing for the salvation of the earth.
They were dancing to wake us up.
And I did wake up. And I know you are awake too.

In fact, I hope the whole world will wake up,
Wake up and join the dance
Join the spirits of the earth, join the salvation of life.

THE HOOP OF NATIONS

On that day, on that wonderful day,
The sun will be shining in the morning sky
The breeze will be fresh with the scent of rain
And the trees will stand waiting like footmen
In their coats of green.

Then a shout of joy will begin,
On the far side of the earth it will begin
And ring right round the world,
Until all of the tribes of all living things
Will be crying out together, crying out in glad adoration.

Peace will have come at last,
Peace in every way for every living thing.
A peace that will never again be broken.

On that day Mother Earth will receive her redemption.
The ancestors will walk with us once again.
The hoop of the nations will be mended.

It will be a day unlike any other.
Not since the first star was born

Was there ever a day like the one that will come
When the Spirit gathers all of creation
As a mother gathers her young.

PRAYER ON A SUMMER EVENING

Out praying in the summer evening.
The heat comes off the ground. It holds me to the earth.

The sky turns purple.
Streaks of yellow and orange
Stain the western edge of the world.
The air barely moves.

The first stars, lazy in the heat,
Make a reluctant appearance
While the moon keeps watch
Without ever changing expression.

I feel a great sense of peace.
A reassurance given without hesitation.
A promise made by a heart that has never known deceit.
A blessing ordained with a touch that heals.

The answer to my prayer is a message for everyone.
Do not be anxious or afraid. Do not feel alone or forgotten.
Do not doubt or despair.
The Spirit is with you.

You will feel the sacred enfold you.
You will be renewed in the vision that has guided you.
You will discover a path you need
And the sources of your support
Will both surprise and comfort you.

A message given and received
On a still summer evening.

NIGHT WATCH

Just before the sun leaves the sky,
In the long lavender light,
you can catch a glimpse of them.

You need to be out in the countryside,
Away from the city glare.
Then if you look to the high places,
The hilltop or the mesa, you may see them
Only for a moment, standing along the horizon.

They are the sentinel spirits,
The ancestors who keep the night watch.
Each evening they take their places,
Appearing as quietly as the stars.
These are our guardian spirits.
These are our elders of eternity.

If you listen, just at moonrise,
You may hear them sing, for only a moment
The night chant, to shelter the earth,
To keep the many tribes of life safe
Until the distant morning.

When you lay your head down and whisper your prayers,
Never be afraid
For the ones who love you are keeping watch,
Their hearts beating in time with your own.

ONE DAY SOON

One day, justice will come running over those hills
Like the wind chasing wildflowers.
It will come to every person who has ever felt belittled,
And nothing will be able to stop it.
It will clean the ancient air like sunlight after a long rain
Reaching down with golden fingers
To make the valley below shine like heaven.

One day love will race around that corner,
Looking for you, looking for me.
It will lift us up in its arms and swing us
Like children pretending to fly.
We will know joy from that day forward forever.

One day the Spirit will come down
From the far mountains
Trailing clouds like a shawl,
Healing the earth with every step.
Then the forests will start to sing,
The deserts will awaken the drum
And our ancestral stars
Will begin their slow and stately dance.

Peace will come to our Mother
And freedom to all her family.
One day, I pray, one day soon.

THE NEXT LIFE

The endless tomorrow stretches out before you.
It is the most beautiful landscape you have ever seen.
It is the forever promised long ago
In so many faith traditions around the world.

Our ancestors have told us over and over again
That there is an existence beyond the one we inhabit
A different place, a better place
Where we will find a new way of living waiting for us.

There are many different ways among us
To envision that new way of being alive
But the belief that it is there is common among us all.
And it has been for millennia.

Like a snow-capped mountain in the human journey
There is a landmark of spiritual wisdom:
Awareness is not an accident.
Life is not just a dignified walk to the grave
But a process of transcendence
That makes graves into doorways
Transforms loss into homecoming
And embodies hope into something you can touch

Because, yes, just as you imagined,
It is as real as you are.
It is the next life. The eternal life.
The life of the world to come.

A PLACE WITHOUT FENCES

I have an appeal to make, Great Spirit,
On behalf of all who will join me:
Please let heaven be somewhere wild and wonderful,
Not tame, not easy
But a place without fences,
A land with mysteries to discover.

Once we pass the threshold of time, please, Spirit
Do not let us find a reality padded by comfort,
But an open space, a free space
Stretching out in prairies and sky,
Desert mesas and ancient forests
Wide blue seas and strong winds
To chase the clouds around.

Let us share this wild world with creatures as alive as us
The flyers and swimmers and runners and climbers,
Our spirit siblings,
Our teachers and guides.

Let us join our ancestors
In a place of earth and rain, of dawn and dusk
Of waterfall and canyon,
So we may live where things can be planted
Take root, and grow again, forever.

FOREVER IS RIGHT BEFORE YOU

When evening comes to the prairies, it comes slowly.

The sun falls through the immense open sky
Drifting down toward the yellow grasslands
Igniting the ochre and orange fire
That burns against the deep purple of twilight.

The colors spread as if moved by an invisible brush
The glow of autumn painted on the vault of heaven.
To stand alone before the failing light
Is to come to the edge of time.

What is past and what will come mingle in the darkness.
Hope peers through the clouds.
The quiet of life is touched only by the wind
Skating over the grass. This is Spirit country.
This is where forever is right before you
In the cooling earth and the burning sky.

IV
BALANCE
OF LIFE

TAKE THE WHEEL AND HOLD IT STEADY

From a wooden longhouse to an underground kiva
To a dance ground on the earth beneath the stars.
Native culture worships in many different ways.
But on one thing our people agree:
These ceremonies are all vital
To keep this world in balance.

Worship is the physical gyroscope
For a cosmic equilibrium.
Harmony does not occur by itself
But by the active participation
Of all the tribes of the human beings.

It does not matter where or how we worship,
But it does matter that we do worship.
And with a common intention:
That life comes into alignment
With the sacred
And that peace be restored among humankind.

There is worship-work to do!
So when the world seems chaotic
When logic and reason are scarce
And when stability is needed like rain in the desert:
Help take the wheel and hold it steady.

LIFE IS A GYROSCOPE

Creation is a carefully calibrated series of balancing acts.
The natural world exists and grows as the earth
Is constantly seeking an environmental equilibrium.

In human life balance is equally important.
We mature as we recognize the role balance
Plays in our lives.
In physical health and emotional well-being
Balance becomes an intuitive response.

My ancestors understood a fundamental principle:
Life is a gyroscope.
As long as we stay in balance,
We can navigate almost anything.

FORGIVENESS ON THE STAIRS

Guilt and I are old friends
Having spent many long hours together.

Guilt tells me how worthless I am.
I confess new and deeper faults.

In the end guilt leaves, promising to return.
I wave farewell, glad guilt is gone

But I am too tired to move.
I slouch toward my bed.

But just as I reach the stairs
Spirit's forgiveness comes bounding down

Childlike with innocent acceptance
Leaps into my arms and makes my soul weightless.

JOYFUL DEFIANCE

Let's slip out the side door of sorrow
Round past the watchman of worry
And make for the green fields beyond.

Let's imagine these frail bodies can dance.
Let's believe we have all we need and more to spare.

It is not pretense but an act of joyful defiance
Against all that would hem the heart
All that would constrain the love within.

Come slip out the side door
To find the peace that waits
In the green fields of faith
Beside streams of distant laughter.

JUSTICE NEVER BENDS TO FEAR

Beware of any generation that seems lost without a leader.
That search may become a dangerous thing to do.

A society that is fearful, money-worried
Anxious for order, hungry for law
A nation of wall builders, accustomed to war
Watching enemies without and enemies within
Afraid its glory will fade:

Longing for the strongman grows, ever so quietly
While people look the other way.

Help us, O Spirit,
Not to flirt with forces so ancient and so evil.
Rather let us put our trust in you
That justice never bends to fear
Nor freedom to false gods of power.

START FEELING

Stop thinking. Start feeling.

If you are wrestling with a problem and it is winning
If you are weighing the evidence
Until you have broken the scale
If you have analyzed the analysis you just analyzed
Then this playful word may be of use:
Stop thinking, start feeling.

There is a loving presence that wants to help
If you will trust the intuition given to you as a child.

Feel the nearness of God.
Feel God's strength surround you.
Feel God's healing power touch you.
Feel, so you may think more clearly.

THE STEADY ART

Patience is not so much a gift as a skill.
It does not come unbidden
As though it were foreign to our nature
But rather it grows through practice
A steady art, made stronger by being so often tested.

Few disciplines are as important.
Few tools of the spiritual life more effective.

Patient in our own struggle
Patient in the need of others.

Patient in our waiting

Patient in our doing
Patient in our receiving.

Patience is how we learn.
Patience is how we become grace.

Patience: the peace of God embodied.

OUR UNEASY AGE

We live in an uneasy age
When doubt urges greed to claim what it can
And confidence fades
As the old temples go unattended.

Public leaders walk backward
As if the past is what we should become.
Distraction is big business.
Information outsells wisdom.

Technology is the magic on which we rely.
You and I were born to this time,
Though we feel no part of it.
We are here to witness to the quiet prophecy of reason
The healing of sharing,
The hope that does not fear the future.

We are stewards of a faith that is not anxious.
We are peace when peace is hard to find.

I WILL CONJURE LOVE

Today I will conjure love from the empty air.
I will call it out from thin places

Where people walk without breathing
From dark places where they stumble without seeing.

I will find love in those I do not like
And let love appear in the faces I avoid.

I will make room for love in my life
Even if I feel overcrowded with worry.

I will offer love without restraint
Even if I have not received love in return.

I will dance with love in innocent pleasure.
I will sing love as though love were a new discovery.

Today I will be the love Spirit made me be
When Spirit loved me from the empty air.

OPEN

Open is a word that goes well with faith.
Open-minded to the new lessons you may teach us
About the mysteries of life.
Open-hearted in compassion to one another
Without the need to judge.
Open-handed in our willingness to help and share
In the work that must be done.
Open in our spirits to follow where you lead
With the dreams you weave around us.
Open to welcome any and all
Who come to seek your shelter.
Open to proclaim your peace with joy and with courage.

NEVER PRAYERS

I have some never prayers, Spirit:

Never let me grow too old
To lose the delight of a child's imagination.
Never so disappointed in life
I stop believing each morning is a new beginning.

Never too concerned with my own burdens
To fail to help another.
Never so busy making a living
That I forget what living is about.

Never so certain I have all the answers
That I stop asking the questions.
Never having so much to say
That I cannot be still and listen.

Never so far from you
That I do not hear when you call my name.

GROWING THE SACRED

What we hold sacred, we cherish, we protect, we nurture.

In an ethical vacuum where nothing is sacred
We are likely to abuse what we would otherwise honor.

As the borders of the sacred diminish,
The empire of sorrow expands.
Sin is the negative space of the sacred.
The work of faith is the restoration of the sacred.

We must help others to discover the value of life
In everything around them. We must grow the sacred.
We must fill in the blank spaces with reverence
And the empty spaces with respect.

SCHOOL OF IMAGINATION

Faith is not belief unexamined
But belief born of deep thought
Shaped by reason, guided by experience, given substance
By the listening of the curious intellect
To voices diverse and ideas divergent.

Religion is not the captive of automated hearts
Set to march in silent obedience
Nor the museum of final thoughts
Beyond which no questions may be asked.

It is the forum of the wise and wondrous,
The company of the healed and healers
The school of human imagination,
The blessed community of the Spirit
Gathered in the clear light of the open mind.

LET TRUTH BE TOLD

Let truth be told. Let love be lived.
Let hope be real. Let peace be lasting.

It might be called a mantra,
A sacred saying to roll around in your mind
But I share these words for more than personal use.

These four phrases danced across my prayers
And kept repeating themselves:
A quiet chant for all of us who live in anxious times.

Please accept my invitation to pray them today
Before the sun sets where you are.
It is our common call to heal the world around us.

Let truth be told. Let love be lived.
Let hope be real. Let peace be lasting.

COME DOWN EASY

Come down easy, dear soul,
Come down easy into the rest you need.

Here is the place prepared for you,
A quiet spot in the midst of the swirl of life
A still pool, where you can be undisturbed and at peace.

Let your worries drift away like autumn smoke.
The world will wait for you,
But for now it is on the far side of the hill.

Your only task is to be healed of impatient time,
Unburdened by demanding thought,
Free of the daily dance of any expectation.
This is the timeless place
The healing place for which you have longed.

Come down easy and stay as long as you like.

CURIOUS

I am not as certain as I am curious.

There are some things I feel certain about
But there are many more things about which I am curious.

That's a good balance.
I want my faith to be an exploration.
I want to stretch my mind as much as comfort my soul.

I like wondering about the how and why of creation.
I have learned a lot from people
With whom I thought I disagreed.
I have discovered new realms of faith
I never even knew were there.

So I pray that I may be forgiven for what I get wrong
But never stop searching for what might be right.

BECAUSE I HAVE BEEN THERE

I have made it through some hard times in my life.
I imagine you have too.

Looking back, I can honestly say
That in more than one of those times
I was not sure I would make it.

The presence of a living and conscious love
Got me through.
I can only call it Spirit.
So my faith is not the product of an emotional need
Or an intellectual imagining.

I believe because I know. Because I have been there.
Because of my experience.

I cannot convince others of this truth.
I can only share it and wait to see
The light of memory in their eyes.

UNTIL THE LIGHT RETURNS

If this is a difficult time for you or for someone you know
Let me speak a clear word straight to your heart:
There is no trouble stronger than the love of the Spirit.

There is no illness, no broken relationship,
No financial setback, no personal hurt
That the love of the Spirit cannot heal.
Not even death can overcome it.

That love is for you.
It may come to you as you read these words
Or it may take time, but it will come to you:

The assurance, the comfort,
The renewal of a love that will embrace you
And hold you and abide with you,
Until the light returns and departs no more.

THE WISDOM WITHIN

Turn to the wisdom within.
Seek out what you have learned over years of experience.
Be guided by these lessons from life.
Study them well and remember what you have recorded
In the heart of your memory.

We each have a story to tell.
We have paid the tuition of our learning
With long nights and difficult days to learn what we value.
We have made discoveries that delighted us.
We have closed some doors we will never want to open.
Ask the Spirit about what to do,
But turn to the wisdom within to know how to do it.

CURMUDGEONS OF JOY

They say as you get older you get more set in your ways.
That's all right with me. I am getting set in my ways.
In fact, I am getting downright stubborn.

I refuse to believe that greed will triumph over justice
That racism is an incurable social disease
That hunger and poverty cannot be overcome
That our planet cannot be restored as a garden of life.

I am stubborn in my faith and optimism.
I am tenacious in love, constant in compassion
Unwavering in my ability to laugh, especially at myself.

I hope many of you are getting set in these ways too.
Let us be the curmudgeons of joy.

HOW WELL WE LOVE

Bend your heart toward love,
As a flower bends to face the sun.

When all is said and done,
The only true measure of our lives
Is how well we loved.
How well we gave love, received love, shared love,
Protected love, created love.

Nothing else will matter when our turn comes
To make the final journey—
Only the love we were will linger.
Only love will still speak our name
In the hearts of those we embraced.

We were made to love, you and I,
Made so by the author of love
Made in the image of love to be the love we are.

NO DEADLINE

We live in a world of time limits, limited offers,
Expiration dates, cut-off points.
And yet our lives rarely work that way.

They are not always so neat and tidy,
Running by the precision of a stopwatch.
Things come up, things change.
We get distracted by other needs
Called away suddenly to take care of other business.

And truthfully, we sometimes put things off,
Afraid to face them, and live in denial.
With the Spirit there are no deadlines,
And for that I am very grateful.
The wonderful grace of the Spirit
Is that there is always an eleventh hour for mercy.

Forgiveness is available long past the date
When we should have asked for it.
The Spirit's love is open all night.

DON'T BE AFRAID

Don't be afraid.

Not you who live alone, not you who struggle with illness
Not you who are walking toward forever, don't be afraid.
Not you, or me, or any of us, we don't have to be afraid.

The beauty within us will never fade
The dreams we have will not disappear
The awareness we call ourselves
Will not simply go out like a light.

What we sense within us,
What we believe we feel around us,
What we have understood as children: all of that is real.
The good is real. The holy is real.

There is a love beyond the scope of our language
That knows each one of us by name.
Don't be afraid.
Love like that does not know how to say goodbye.

WHAT HAS ALWAYS BEEN THERE

We are forgiven for the mistakes we have made.
We are loved without condition.
We are blessed without asking.
We are watched over when we are careless.
We are understood when we are not making sense.
We are remembered
Even when we have forgotten ourselves.

The reality in which we live is conscious.
The world we inhabit is aware.

The Spirit around us is compassion.
We may not understand it all.
We may differ widely in how we describe it.
But we each have an invitation to freedom
A chance to see more deeply, a path to follow home.
We awaken to what is sacred. We grow into the holy.
We find what has always been there.

PRAYER IS HOW I BREATHE

People have asked me, since I pray so much
Do I ever get discouraged or doubtful
Because not all my prayers are answered.
No, and for lots of reasons.

For me, prayer is not a gumball machine
Where I put in my quarter and take out my prize.
Because I am not a puppet on a string
I cannot pull on that string to get some attention.

The natural state of prayer is mystery.
I only know that I am born into a life
Where I am fragile and finite.
I believe there is a conscious presence
Around me that cares for me.
I offer my thanks and my hopes.
I feel and see the response.
That response is always loving.
So prayer is how I breathe: Spirit is the air.

RHYTHM OF KINDNESS

True humility is a reflex.
Like the blinking of an eye, it happens automatically.
It is not planned or postured but occurs instinctively.

When we have so deeply internalized the spiritual value
That all people are to be loved without exception
And that we are to be the natural embodiment of that love
Then we behave with a sense of respect
That is effortless and unconscious.

We would gladly serve persons of any walk of life
Even those far different from ourselves
Because by so doing we become the heartbeat of God:
A constant rhythm of kindness
That never discriminates and never judges.

HOUSE OF THE SPIRIT

Rest well now, for you are safe in the hands of the Spirit.
Do not be fretful over what you have yet to do
Or anxious over what you have done in the past.

You are in the Spirit's time
A place of forgiveness for what has been
And hope for what is to come.

You are in sheltered space
A quiet haven where old hurts are healed
And fresh dreams are conjured
Watched over by angels who walk the silent halls
Keeping vigil over your slumber
Until they open the shutters of vision to your new day.

Rest well, for you are in the house of the Spirit
The home of peace and patience.

MY SPIRITUAL JOB DESCRIPTION

Practice justice: withhold judgment.

I have been keeping that small equation before me
As a way to maintain spiritual balance.
So often it is easier to judge others
Than do the hard work of justice.

Even many religious communities seem to spend
More time pointing fingers than extending hands.

So whenever I am tempted to blame other people
I try to let this little mantra remind me
Of my spiritual job description.

I am not a judge but an advocate.
My task is not to condemn others
But to find a path to community with them
No matter how difficult that work may be.

NO HARM

No harm to those in danger's way,
No harm to the innocent and the frail,
No harm to the poor,
No harm to families gathered round their children

No harm to field or forest,
No harm to mystics and dreamers,
No harm to creatures great or small,
No harm to those who work for justice

No harm to the makers of beauty,
No harm to those of any faith,
No harm to those with no faith,
No harm to heaven or to earth

No harm to you, no harm to me
For this day, as far as my prayer can reach,
No harm, no harm at all.

PRAYER FOR THOSE WHO WAIT

Waiting is the hard part.

Waiting for the results of medical tests.
Waiting for a loved one to come home.
Waiting on the call for a new job.

There are a thousand waiting rooms in our lives
A place of uncertainty, anxiety, even fear.
If and when you are in this place
Let this prayer support you:

Please, Spirit of mercy, be with me as I wait.
Don't leave me alone in this empty space
But fill it with your presence.
Remind me that I am not alone.
Give me strength to let time pass as it must.
Stand by me until the waiting is over
And stay with me whatever the outcome may be.

AGILE SPIRITS

Sometimes we move forward by standing still.
There are moments in life when simply staying quiet
Or holding our ground is the best choice we can make.

Sometimes our progress is in turning around
Changing the direction in which we are heading
Recognizing a dead end when we see it.

Sometimes we are called to make a bold advance
Stepping out of the crowd to take responsibility
Daring the consequences for the sake of justice.

My ancestors taught that we live
Within a spiritual gyroscope.
We are not static beings,
One dimensional in thought and action
But agile spirits seeking balance and direction.

I KNOW I AM NOT ALONE

I will not be silenced by those who shout.
I will not bow my head to those
Who hold theirs high with arrogance.

I will not move for those who push the poor aside.
I will not sit down when justice calls us all to stand.

I am not particularly brave
And I do not think I am always right.
I am willing to listen and learn
But I am not willing to deny what I believe.

I will not accept hate over love
Or oppress others for the sake of privilege.
I believe we are all equal
And we all deserve to be treated with dignity.

I have enough faith in the future
To be willing to change the present.
I am only one, but I know I am not alone.

FEAR LIKES TO BLUFF

I have played poker with fear before
Waiting to see which cards would fall
Judging my bets by my faith
Keeping as calm as I could
Even if my heart was pounding
Staying in the game
Eye to eye with what scared me
Not willing to fold
Because the stakes were so high.

I have not always won every hand.
Life is a gamble.
But I have won enough to know
Fear can be beaten.
Fear likes to bluff
To win with nothing to show
But a good poker face.

I am no card shark
But I will not let fear take it all
Even if I am the last player at the table.
Fear is a loser as long as I keep my cool.

A SPIRITUAL FINDER

Like you, I have thought of myself as a spiritual seeker.
And while that is true for me,
Its logical outcome is equally true:
I am a spiritual finder.

That realization helps to balance
The reality of my spiritual quest.
Yes, I am seeking new discoveries and new ideas.
Yes, I have gained some insights
And taken some positions along the way.
But if I am only a seeker I can skip over
The need to embrace what I believe.

As a finder I pitch my tent of faith
On the ground of my beliefs.
Before the journey continues, I need to say:
Here is where I start.
If you are also out looking,
You will know where to find me.

BLESSED ARE THE GOOFY

I wish there were a benediction that said,
Blessed are the goofy.
That would work for me.

I have done some pretty amazingly goofy things in my life
And despite my best efforts,
I imagine I will do some more.
Nothing harmful, mind you, just goofy. Just a little odd.
One of those "what was I thinking?" episodes.

Fortunately, the Spirit is prepared for people like me.
There is a contingency plan in heaven that covers goofiness
A special dispensation for those of us
Who need a little extra help
For our good intentions that didn't work out so well.
So relax. Goofy is not contagious—
Although it is hereditary.

GO WILD

Go wild once in a while.
Go rogue.
Do something outrageous and unexpected
Something fun and fanciful
Throwing caution
And a lot of other things
Your mother always told you
To the wind.

Scandalize the prim and proper set
Take a chance on your own imagination
Your own sense of direction
Testing the limits of how far you can fly
When the wind is at your back
The world before you open with possibilities
And the people who told you
You would never get off the ground
Are far, far behind you.

Go wild once in a while.

BLUE-COLLAR BELIEVERS

I have a new description for some of us:
Spiritual pragmatists.
We are definitely not pessimists
Because we do not always expect something bad to happen
Having seen the good emerge
Where and when least expected.

But we are not strictly optimists, because we know
We are up against some long odds and don't always win.
But we never lose faith. And we never give up hope.
So we put some sweat equity into what we believe.

We work at creating justice.
We try again. We keep going.
We are spiritual pragmatists
Blue-collar believers busy building a dream.

WE ARE THE DESIGNERS OF MEMORY

One of our most important spiritual jobs
Is to make memories.

Our task is to help those for whom we care
To increase the number of memories that make them smile
Make them feel appreciated,
Make them know they are loved.

We do this in many different ways,
Some complex, some simple
But all made with our unique touch.
We are the designers of memory.

We are the architects of experiences that last
Moments so happy or so kind that they are transformed
Into the longest-lasting possession
Any human being can have: a memory
That may be with a person to the day they die.

In the end, the memories we make
Are our most enduring achievement.

DON'T LOOK AWAY

Don't look down, don't look back, don't look away.

Don't look down with your head bent by sorrow or fear
For the courage you have within you is reason enough
To hold your head high.

Yes, you carry a heavy burden,
But you know you never carry it alone.
Look up, for love still has much to show you.

Don't look back to the old hurts and struggles
For they have had their moment
And cannot live in the light of this new day.

Look ahead to what life offers you now.
Don't look away from the challenges before you
No matter how hard they may seem.

Breathe in the strength of the Spirit
And trust what guides you.
Look your truth straight in the eye
And capture the vision that will set you free.

FALSE STARTS

If it is true that we learn from our mistakes
I must be a genius because I have made so many.

I am living proof that when you try,
You do not fail, only learn.
I have started down a dozen paths
Before I discovered the right one.
I have begun work on many projects of hope
Only to have to back up and try again.

My false starts and mistakes
Are not reasons for me to hang my head
But proof that persistence,
Experience, and vision really do pay off over time.

Do not be afraid of ideas that don't work.
They are only there to lead you to the ones that do.

SPIRITUAL OR STUBBORN

I don't know if I am spiritual or stubborn
Or maybe a combination of both
But the more the bad news piles up
The more determined I am to respond to it
With the good news I feel so clearly in my mind and heart.

Yes, life is hard. It is full of suffering and sorrow
And believe me, I have had my fair share.
But life is also beautiful, full of moments
That are transcendent in their healing and love.
I know because I have been blessed
By more of them than I can count.

I cannot change the reality of pain or loss
But I can claim the reality of grace and joy.
Maybe I am just stubborn
But I do not want my last word to be a complaint
But an alleluia.

NO CHARGE FOR REDEMPTION

Yes, of course you can be forgiven
Forgiven for the mistakes you have made
Forgiven for the things you most deeply regret.

You can be restored to the integrity of your life.
You can be renewed and made whole again
At peace and with a deeper sense of hope
Than you ever imagined was possible.

And the cost for this level of redemption?

No charge. No obligation.
Just a willingness to be honest with yourself
And with others.
The courage to see the truth
And the sincerity to make it right again.
The Spirit will do the rest.

FAR SIDE OF THE MOON

I have fallen off the edge of the world.
I have traveled the far side of the moon.
I have known sorrow and loss,
Wandering the back streets of hope.

But never have I been away from the love of the Spirit.

It has followed me, sheltered me, protected me,
And kept me alive more than once.

No matter how hard your life may become
Please believe that you are not on your own
But watched over by eyes
That never look away and never close.

The love of the Spirit is constant.
The mercy of the Spirit is endless.
And the Spirit will find you when you are lost
Even on the far side of the moon.

SPIRITUALITY IS A TOOLBOX

Some people may think that spirituality
Has the depth of a greeting card
All happy wishes and sweet sentiments
But in fact, as most of us who have faith can tell you
Spirituality is a toolbox for hard times
More than a basket of flowers.

Our faith informs our understanding
Of the difficult ethical issue.
It guides us through conflict, not away from it.
It helps us to face hardship, illness, and death.
It teaches us deep lessons
In human relationships and justice.

Spirituality requires courage, discipline,
And a willingness to listen and learn.
It is what life looks like when you not only believe in hope
But build it.

JOY AWAKENS US

I have seen enough of sadness to know the meaning of joy.
It is not a feeling but a liberation.

Joy is a spiritual gift,
The full expression of the love at the center of life.
It suddenly appears within us,
In a flash of realization that hope is real.

Joy awakens us. It reveals how powerful happiness can be
When it is in its most pure and healing form.

I give thanks for the possibility of joy in our lives
No matter how rare it may be.

For as long as we can experience joy
We can step out of any shadows
Reality may wrap around us like a shroud.

Joy is how we began and how we will end:
In the delight of being who we are.

YOUNG IN WONDER

I think I got this backward:
I thought when people got older
They became more settled in their ways.
More conservative and careful.
Less inclined to go out searching for something new.

But I seem to have become the opposite.

I am more of a spiritual nomad than ever
Out exploring the mysteries around me.
I am sure I have a home in the Spirit
But I cannot stop looking out the window.
The night sky looks like a roadmap
The first light of dawn like an invitation.
I see other seekers already heading for the unknown
And I long to be with them.

We are a community old in experience
But young in wonder.

MY BEST-LAID PLANS

Now that I am a little older,
I realize I have misplaced my best-laid plans.
I know I put them down somewhere,
But for the life of me I cannot remember where.

Which may be just as well
Since most of my long-range plans
Took off like a cement airplane.
I think my current strategy of smiling a lot
Is working out much better.

It causes some people to assume that I know something.
So as long as I don't say anything
And remove all doubt I should be fine.

I hope your own cunning plan is going well too.
Knowing you, I am sure it is a doozy.
(And if you are around my age,
I hope you can remember where you put your doozy.)

GUMPTION

The farm side of my family would have called it
Spiritual gumption.
That word isn't heard much these days,
But when I was small the old-timers used it a lot.

He or she has got gumption, they would say;
And it was meant as a compliment.
A great compliment,
Because gumption was all about having character.

Gumption was resilience, determination, and creativity.
It meant you would not fold up or quit,
Even if the going got hard.

It was a matter of confidence, the good kind
That comes from a life lived in faith and dignity.

So let me say to everyone that I am proud of you
Proud to be a part of you,
Because you have spiritual gumption
Just when we need it the most.

THE LAND OF REGRET

I have visited the land of regret more than once
But have never lived there, for the land is barren
And no person would make their home there

Unless, as the elders say, they have been so focused
On their sorrow and shame
That they have lost their way to forgiveness
The sacred well in any desert

Lost their way to repentance and reconciliation
So they haunt the wild lands of their own memory
Seeking responsibility like a mirage.

Better, the elders say, to let regret do its job:
Be a teacher with a lesson that must be learned.

Then make your cairn to mark your passing
To express your regret, to accept the teaching
And walk on, keeping to the straight path before you.

A SOUL ON LOAN

We will not grow old, not in spirit.

In mind and body, yes, we will age as all things age
All making the pilgrimage
Through time to find the place of sources.

But in our spirit, no, we will not grow old.

The child that was us will run forever through the fields.
The dreams we spun from the fine wool of cloud watching
Will forever lead us to the next wonder that awaits us.

The love we knew, so quiet, so life giving
Will always be there to lift us up and hold us close.

The spirit of life is eternal. It does not diminish.
It does not forget. It does not alter.

The spirit within us is the sum total
Of our sacred experience.
It is what we were sent here to be and to do.

Our spirit, a soul in transit, has a life outside of time.
It will not grow old because it is on loan
From a source more ancient than time itself.

LET YOUR LIFE BEGIN

Let your life begin again, and let it begin today.
Let truth pass into you with all of its healing grace
An acknowledgment of what has been done
A door, not a cage
An invitation to a fresh start on a path already begun.

Stand and walk, out into the world around you
Back into the broad valleys of your own heart
Feeling life renewed with every step you take.

You are not bound, you are not broken
You are free and you are whole.
Rise on the air that streams to heaven.

Put on your faith, put on your hope.
Smile to welcome whatever comes.
For this day your life begins again
And will each day forever.

I WILL LOOK BACK

I know the seasons of life and I understand
The impermanence of all things
But that doesn't make it any easier.

I will miss this mess, one day.

I will hear my name being called by my ancestors
And I will turn my face
To the fresh air of the world to come
But I will look back. I know I will look back.

Life is not so bad when you think of how many things
Go into the making of it.
Morning light, sea breezes, gardens after the rain.
The routines we create to make our life give us comfort
When life is not being easy at all.

The memories that have already become sacred to us
And the monuments of our hearts
To the great struggles we endured.
We will turn back to see it, all of it, one last time.

However grand, however difficult: it was our home.
And that's why I love it, all of it,
All of life in all of its ways of being alive
With every breath given and every blessing received.

SECRET LANGUAGE OF THE HEART

I know the secret language of the heart
How it speaks in whispers about the pain it has known

How it talks of loves lost and dreams deferred,
The wordless memories of a lifetime

Sharing a story that cannot be contained by words
But expressed only in the sound of rain.

It is the collective sound of all those voices
All those stories, all those moments of joy
That I seek to raise up to the listening skies

To hold up as high as I can in prayer
That the angels of the night will hear us
All of us with the dignity of our own story

And know that we are still here, still together
Still doing what we can to make hope have meaning.

Keep speaking the poetry of your heart.
I am listening. Many of us are listening.
We do not need language to tell the same story.

WE'LL MANAGE

Coming from a family that was not to the manor born
I understood that my parents had to work hard
To keep us going.

Sometimes things got a little tight in the family budget.
That's when I would hear them say the two words
That have helped me so much through life.
What are the two words? "We'll manage."

That's what I heard so often: we'll manage.
I like the plainness of it, the pragmatic honesty.
It does not pretend things won't be difficult.
It doesn't seek to put on a brave face.
It just announces the simple confidence
Of hard-working people
That they will find a way to make it work.

So much of the spirit of any people is their ability
To look at an uncertain tomorrow and believe
They will find their way forward.
So don't worry. We'll manage.

THE FIFTH
DIRECTION

LET THE WHEELS TURN

Let the wheels turn, Spirit, let them turn.
Wheels of truth, wheels of justice, let them turn.
Even if it pains us to see what they show.
Even if it deepens our sorrow or our shame
Let them turn, for we know that we will never move
Beyond this point unless they take us there.

We cannot ignore our past or avoid our present.
We must confront them both as clearly
And as honestly as we can.
We must see the depth
And breadth of the challenge before us.
We will not survive as one people
Living in two separate realities.
We must turn to face what is real,
Whether we like the look of it or not.

So let the wheels turn,
Wheels of truth and wheels of justice,
Let them do their work
Openly, carefully, until they begin to create
The transparent foundation of our new community.
Prevent any hand from seeking

To stop their progress, Spirit,
For in the light of truth and in the integrity of justice
We will find the unity that we need
To restore peace to our land.

I began this book with an introduction of myself as a descendant of the Trail of Tears. In the 1830s Andrew Jackson forced my ancestors off their land. In doing so, he violated the Constitution of the United States and ignored the ruling of the Supreme Court. It is a moment of dictatorship in American history that is little talked about and largely forgotten, except among those of us whose lives were profoundly damaged by the results.

We lost everything. Land. Tradition. Kinship. Vision. Balance. We lost it all in the long march from our ancestral homeland, Chahta Yakni, to the exile waiting for us in a strange place we called Okla Homma, "Red People," the refugee camp for all of our Indigenous relatives who would soon be sent on death marches like we had been.

We had lost contact with the Four Directions. We had lost the graves of our ancestors and the tradition those graves enshrined. We had seen the kinship of our clans destroyed as people were scattered and forced to change their names to English. We had lost our balance and equilibrium as a society. We had even lost our ancient vision, our faith in justice and mercy. The effort to exterminate us, to practice cultural genocide against us, was almost complete. The greed and cruelty of our oppressors seemed triumphant.

Then something mysterious happened.

Huddled as strangers in a strange land, cut off from all that had sustained us for thousands of years, stripped of every resource that could restore our dignity as a people, we slowly discovered the miracle of the Fifth Direction.

Like all miracles, it is hard to define, even hard to describe this holy revelation. It transcends our logic and reason. By every measure of destruction we should have been wiped out, left to linger in poverty and degradation until we disappeared into the footnotes of colonialism's evil history. The "Vanishing Americans," they called us.

But we did not vanish. We survived. Against all the odds we survived. Denied access to the Four Directions, my ancestors slowly turned toward the one direction remaining—the timeless, transcendent direction of the Spirit. This direction defies the descriptions of north and south, east and west, up and down, in and out. It is a sacred direction, a leap of faith. The Fifth Direction is an act of trust so profound that it is walking on water, stepping out over the void with no bridge visible beneath our feet.

The Fifth Direction is like a resurrection. It is life overcoming death. It is contrary to all the physics of our reality, a suspension of the rules by which we operate, a sudden intervention of a power beyond our comprehension. This level of faith is difficult for the comfortable and privileged to imagine. Those padded by their own sense of power and confident in their own pride can hardly conceive that the old dreams of the mystics could really come true: that some great divine force could actually come to earth and alter our reality at will.

But when you hurt, when you are broken, when you are stripped bare and left to die: suddenly that possibility becomes your only option. Your only hope. Your only faith. A miraculous restoration may seem a subject of derision for those who have never known a Trail of Tears. But for those who have experienced that, a miracle is the opening up of a new dimension of reality. A Fifth Direction transforms life through the intervention of the Spirit.

Do I believe this is true?

Absolutely, for I have seen it many times over. I have seen it in the stories of countless Indigenous cultures that have faced genocide. I have seen it in communities that have survived slavery. I have seen it in individual lives, when all hope for healing was gone and only death could be expected to have the last word. I have seen it in a man who was an alcoholic and dying on the floor of a dingy motel. The hand that created these miracles may be unseen, but the tracks left by the Spirit are there for all to see.

No matter how much we think we are in charge, no matter how vain we may become in our technology and our power, no matter how little we believe in a higher power: there come clear moments when our strength fails and only that unseen hand remains to hold us up. To heal us. To restore us. To make the Four Directions turn once again on the Spirit Wheel.

Why am I telling you all of this? For the same reason I write my little messages every day.

I want you to be aware of the reality of the sacred. I want you to believe in the Spirit. I want you to have a link to the Fifth Direction. You may call the Spirit by any name you choose. You may believe and pray as seems right to you. I am not out to convert you to any one tradition, but rather to recruit you to count yourself among those of us who have seen the Fifth Direction at work in the world around us. I want you to do that, because in the days to come we are going to need that holy intervention, perhaps more than we have ever needed it before.

If you read my words, you know I am not a prophet of doom and gloom. My sense of hope is built on the rock of my faith. But I am a wise enough elder to watch the sky for signs of change. Good change and bad change. And I see those signs all around me. I see them coming toward us. And I am betting you do too.

Like me, you watch the painful suffering of Mother Earth. Like me, you see the bonds of kinship among human beings crack and break apart. Like me, you watch more people lose their vision and turn away from belief in anything greater than themselves. Like me, you see the world get out of balance and descend into fear and war. These are all signs that we are going on a long march together, a forced migration into a future we can neither control nor predict. We will have sent ourselves on this journey through darkness, but we will not be able to turn back from where it is taking us. At some moment our strength will be expended. Our technology will not save us. Our money will not buy our freedom. Our power will not protect us.

Only an intervention of the Spirit—that miraculous Fifth Direction—will halt the decline and return us to joy. And I believe that intervention will occur when we all acknowledge our need for it. Not just one of us. Not just a particular tribe or nation. Not just one faith community. But all of us: people from every culture, every religion, every continent. When enough of us, on a global scale, are willing to make spiritual peace with our neighbors, practice justice and compassion toward other human beings of every walk of life, and turn our technologies toward the health and healing of our Mother Earth and all her children—then balance will be restored, kinship reunited, and a new tradition resurrected into a world at ease with itself.

My messages are wake-up calls to humanity. They are seeds of the Four Directions being planted in every mind and heart they can find. They are the hope that will be the first dawn of the Fifth Direction when we are ready to receive it. The more people who read them, the more people there will be who will hasten the coming of the Spirit. We all have a job to do. We are all needed to spread the word of kindness, acceptance, unity, and compassion. It does not matter what religion we embrace, what language we speak, what culture we call home. It only matters that we accept others as part of the tribe of the human beings and dedicate our own best efforts to create justice and peace among us. We can all send out those messages in our own way, within our own community. In time, they will link up with people in distant places doing exactly the same work. Eventually, our messages will form a global movement for the restoration and reconciliation that we need.

My book ends in mystery.

How can things that have died be brought back to life? How can people who are broken be made whole? How can lost dreams be found? How can the last be first? How can old enemies become new friends?

So many questions and so many mysteries in the long migration we see before us. Is it a place of shadows or light? I do not know, for I am no prophet. I am just an old man who believes in what his own lifetime of experience and learning has taught him: there is a Spirit who loves creation without exceptions and who will be there when needed if only we make room in our hearts to receive that love.

I am only one among many, just like you are. But I am determined to make the destination of this long walk a blessing, not only for me and for my people but for every life on the Spirit Wheel, for every hope that turns beneath the Four Directions.